HAVE YOU EVER WONDERED:

* Why guys are so jealous?
* Why girls always expect guys to spend money?
* How to say no to a guy when you just aren't ready?
* How to start up a conversation with a girl?
* Why guys have such trouble expressing how they feel?
* Why it's so important to say "I love you" to a girl?

These questions and many more are all answered in...

THE OPPOSITE SEX IS DRIVING ME CRAZY

The one sourcebook for teenagers everywhere to discover what boys think about girls and what girls think about boys!

Also by Joyce Vedral
Published by Ballantine Books:

I DARE YOU
MY PARENTS ARE DRIVING ME CRAZY
I CAN'T TAKE IT ANY MORE

Physical Fitness Titles

NOW OR NEVER
SUPER CUT
HARD BODIES

JOYCE L. VEDRAL, Ph.D.

THE OPPOSITE SEX IS DRIVING ME CRAZY

BALLANTINE BOOKS • NEW YORK

Copyright © 1988 by Joyce Vedral, Ph.D.

All rights reserved under International and Pan-American Copyright Conventions. Published in the United States of America by Ballantine Books, a division of Random House, Inc., New York, and simultaneously in Canada by Random House of Canada Limited, Toronto.

Library of Congress Catalog Card Number: 87-91878

ISBN 0-345-35221-1

Manufactured in the United States of America

First Edition: August 1988

– TABLE OF CONTENTS –

Introduction

Part I. What Girls Want to Know About Boys 1

1. —Jealousy and Cheating: Why? 3
2. —Love, Romance, and Relationships: How Boys Feel 12
3. —Arguments: I Say Black—He Says White 26
4. —How Do Boys Feel About Spending Time and Money? 35
5. —How Boys Really Feel About Sex 44
6. —I Can Never Figure Out Why Boys... (Strange Ways of Boys) 57
7. —What Turns a Guy Off? What Turns a Guy On? 67
8. —The Worst Thing I Ever Did to a Girl: Guys' True Confessions 77
9. —What Moms and Dads Tell Their Sons About Girls 85
10. —How to Get and Keep the Guy of Your Dreams 94

Part II. What Boys Want to Know About Girls 97

1. —Jealousy and Cheating: Why? 99
2. —Love, Romance, and Relationships: How Girls Feel 109
3. —Arguments: I Say Black—She Says White! 119
4. —Girls' Attitudes About Spending—Your Time and Your Money 130
5. —How Girls Really Feel About Sex 138
6. —I Can Never Figure Out Why Girls... (Strange Ways of Girls) 150

7.—What Turns a Girl Off? What Turns a Girl On? 161
8.—The Worst Thing I Ever Did to a Guy: Girls' True Confessions 171
9.—What Moms and Dads Tell Their Daughters About Boys 181
10.—How to Get and Keep the Girl of Your Dreams 189
Bibliography 191

– ACKNOWLEDGMENTS –

To Bob Wyatt for loving the idea.

To Simone Cooper for saying: "I can't wait to read it."

To Richard McCoy—for being sharp, efficient, and ever so patient in answering questions, editorial and otherwise.

To Beth Rashbaum for a fine job in editing the manuscript.

To Marthe Simone Vedral, my own teenage daughter, for her innate teenage wisdom and her advice to me, for her willingness to stop what she was doing and help me with various questions that came up during the final writing of the manuscript. "Read this paragraph, Marthe. How does this sound?" And she would sigh, read it, answer me, and then run back to her phone call, or her homework, or whatever.

Thank you—all of the wonderful teenagers from all over the United States who asked and answered the questions in this book, especially the teenagers of Julia Richman High School in New York City and General Douglas McArthur High School on Long Island.

Special thanks to my nephews Jason and Jared Vale.

Thank you, Dory Davidson, chairperson of the English Department of Julia Richman High School, for your dedication to teenagers.

Thank you, Andrew Jones, principal of Julia Richman High School, for providing an excellent role model for teenagers.

Thank you to my mother and father, Martha and Dave Yellin, for the wisdom and guidance you've always provided.

And most important, Thank God. I must have said it or wildly prayed it at least a thousand times during the writing of this book: "Help me, God. What wise advice can I give them on this issue?" But being human, I'm sure I didn't always get the answer exactly right, so please, don't blame God for the faults of this book. He's got enough things being blamed on Him already.

– INTRODUCTION –

There are certain things about guys that drive girls crazy, and there are certain things about girls that drive guys crazy. Girls want to know: "Why is it so hard to get a guy to say 'I love you?'" "Why are guys so possessive?" "Why does my boyfriend act different toward me when he's in front of his friends?" "Why do most guys think it's okay for them to have sex with lots of different partners, yet disrespect girls who do the same?" "What lines do guys use to get a girl into bed?" "Would a guy break up with you just because you refuse to have sex with him?" (Turn to page 18 for an answer to this one.)

Guys want to know: "Why does my girlfriend demand that I spend so much time with her?" "Why is she so jealous?—I can't even talk to another girl." "Why do girls take so long to get dressed?" "Why are girls so romantic?" "What really turns girls on?" "Why does a girl think I'm out for only one thing when I may just want to build a good relationship with her?" (Turn to page 138 right now if you want an answer to this one.)

These and many more questions are answered in this

book—not by me, but by lots of teenagers from all over the United States. I interviewed young adults from New York City; Long Island, New York; Los Angeles, California; Detroit, Michigan; Chicago, Illinois; Miami Beach, Florida; Pittsburgh, Pennsylvania; Boston, Massachusetts; St. Paul, Minnesota; Cleveland, Ohio; and Dallas, Texas. These teenagers range in age from thirteen to nineteen and are a mixture of every race typically found in high schools all around the United States: black, white, Chicano, Puerto Rican, Oriental, etc. These teenagers tell you *exactly* why they say and do the things they say and do.

I've spent a lot of time around teenagers. I have a teenage daughter of my own, teenage nephews, and many teenage friends. I've also spent years as an English teacher in a New York City high school. Lately, I've been meeting teenagers from all over the United States when I've been a guest on television talk shows discussing the books I've written for teenagers on how to get along with parents, how to get out of trouble, how to get out of any kind of depression, etc. (See bibliography for a list of my books.) I also get to find out what teenagers are thinking when I give lectures to teen groups at various high schools, libraries, etc., throughout the United States, because after the lectures, they bombard me with questions—many of them found in this book.

Whenever I meet teenagers, I listen to them talking to each other and complaining about various things. Then I ask myself: "What is their main concern and what can I do to help them?" Recently, as I listened, it became clear that teenagers could use a book about the opposite sex—not a preachy book that tells them how to act, but a book that tells the inside story—why boys and girls act the way they do in the words of the teenagers themselves. In other words, I wanted to write a book that would tell them how the "other half" thinks.

So I wrote this book. After doing all the interviews, I selected the most repeated questions and answers, and then I picked the most interesting and/or humorous ones. If there was only one answer to the contrary and a hundred answers the other way, I dealt with the hundred and not the one. For example, when I asked boys if they wanted to marry a virgin, only one out of more than one hundred said no. So in this book I talked about why boys want to marry virgins (if they can find them . . . as the boys admit).

But I did more than just gather questions and answers from teenagers. After I selected the most common and interesting questions and answers, in keeping with my goal to help you to make your life happier and more fulfilling, I took the opportunity to give you some ideas on what to do with the information you gained from the guys' and girls' answers. In other words, I put my "two cents" into it. I know teenagers well enough by now to realize that that's all it is. Two cents. A small contribution to your total development, but my contribution. Of course, you will decide whether to take it or leave it. I hope you take it or at least think about it.

I had more fun writing this book than any other book I've written so far. I hope you enjoy reading it, too. I'd love to hear from you—either with a response to this book or maybe with a question not covered in this book. You may even want to request that I write a special book for teenagers on a given topic. My only reason for writing another book for teenagers would be to answer a need. "We need a book on . . ." So, if you want to get in touch with me, write to the following address:

Joyce L. Vedral
P.O.B. A 433
Wantagh, New York, 11793-0433

P.S. If you want to know a little more about me, read the About the Author at the end of this book.

Part 1
What Girls Want to Know About Boys

1

Jealousy and Cheating: Why?

Did you ever go out with a jealous guy? You know, the kind of guy who jumps to conclusions even if you're just innocently talking to another boy? Why do guys do this? Or have you had the bad experience of finding out that your boyfriend has been cheating on you all along —maybe even while he's been unjustly accusing you of the things he himself has been doing!

In this chapter boys will tell you what makes them jealous and why they cheat on you. We'll talk about jealousy first.

– I ASSUME THEY'RE TRYING TO PICK HER UP –

One of the most common reasons for boys getting suspicious when their girl is merely talking to another guy is *insecurity*.

> I assume they're trying to pick her up. Then, when I call her and she's not home, I start wondering.
>
> *Joe, 15*

I'm afraid she's going to see something in them that I don't have.

Anthony, 17

I feel threatened when a guy speaks to my girl. I assume she's cheating just in case it winds up being true—it's like keeping my guard up.

Dave, 17

Girls fall in love easy. You can never be too careful.

Tom, 18

Boys don't actually believe you're planning to cheat on them; they're just afraid you might. Of course they're not going to tell you: "I'm not sure I'm man enough to hold on to you. I'm insecure." So instead they behave in a defensive and protective manner—like a dog who starts growling as soon as he sees someone approaching his bone. (No dog waits until his bone is actually being snatched to growl. He sets up a series of loud snarls to ward off the threat so that it will never materialize.) As long as this stays at the growling stage, there's no harm done. Some girls even like a jealous boyfriend, someone to make them feel really wanted—but if it goes beyond that, look out! You don't want to risk violence when you talk to another guy. And you certainly don't want to be made a prisoner.

– I FEEL LIKE A FOOL –

Boys are very self-conscious about what their friends may think, and they worry a lot about how it looks and what it means when their girlfriends seem interested in anyone besides them.

Hanging out with other guys is disrespectful to me—like saying I'm not that important.

Kyle, 16

You don't get jealous. You just look like a fool. Your friends say to you: "You let your girlfriend talk to those guys. That's pretty bad."

John, 18

Why would she have to talk to another boy? If she wants to know anything, she can talk to me.

Sal, 17

Guys are always unsure of their ability to hold the attention of their girlfriends. The male ego is very fragile where this issue is concerned. Perhaps you've heard of the expression "cuckold" or of the symbol of the "horns." Both are used to poke fun at guys who aren't "man enough" to keep their women from going with other men. You can see where more than mere jealousy is involved. This is a question in guys' relationships with each other as well as with their girlfriends.

– SHE WANTS TO MAKE ME JEALOUS –

In some cases, guys think that girls actually provoke them into jealousy. Have you ever done this? Chances are, if you did, your boyfriend knew what you were doing. That makes him not only jealous but angry, too.

My girlfriend *wants* me to get jealous and upset. I could be walking down the street with her and she'll eye some guy and say, "He looks good," but then she'll look at me and laugh and say, "Baby, I'm only kidding." It's very hard to trust her.

Darren, 17

Every girl has her own style of relating to boys. If your style is to keep him wondering, that's your choice to make—but you'll probably have to put up with a suspicious boyfriend, and sometimes that can cause *big* problems—especially if your boyfriend is the violent type.

– I WOULDN'T EXACTLY CALL IT CHEATING –

Do boys cheat? Yes, they do. But why? Girls want to know: "Why do you tell your girlfriend you love her and then cheat on her when she's not around?"

> That's how I enjoy my youth. I like to have other girls to turn to.
>
> *Rico, 15*

> I'm seventeen and I think my relationships with girls are just temporary. Even though I might tell a girl I love her, I feel I still have a love life ahead, and it's too soon to get serious.
>
> *Ray, 17*

> When I say I love her, I'm not lying. But I may love other girls, too. Truthfully, I just like to meet new people. I wouldn't exactly call it cheating.
>
> *Jared, 17*

> I cheat because sometimes my friends persuade me. They say, come on, Tom, the hell with what's-her-face, she'll never find out. Then I don't want to look stupid to my friends, so I do it.
>
> *Tom, 17*

Boys see others because they feel they're too young to limit themselves to one girl—they want to "enjoy their youth." They're not necessarily lying when they tell you they love you, but they also want to be free to see how they feel about others. I don't blame you if you don't like it, but this kind of behavior is perfectly normal for teenagers—girls as well as boys. If you don't explore other relationships now, when will you do it—after you're married?

Many guys cheat just because they feel they're expected to. Tom cheats because he doesn't want his friends to think his girlfriend is controlling him. Teenage boys don't want *that* reputation any more than they want the reputation of being a "cuckold" or getting "the horns." So sometimes they will cheat just to show off and prove to their friends that they are "one of the boys" and are "*in control of* their woman"—not *controlled by* their woman.

– SHE WOULDN'T TELL ME IF SHE WERE DOING IT –

If both boys and girls want to explore—and they do—why don't they just tell each other the truth? What would happen if boys told their girlfriends that they see others? Here's what the boys have to say about why they don't level with their girlfriends.

> I know she'll try to get even with me by doing the same thing.
>
> *Henry, 15*

> She loves me and I wouldn't want to hurt her. That's cruel.
>
> *Tony, 17*

> She wouldn't want to hear that, and besides, she wouldn't tell me if she were doing it.
>
> *Bill, 18*

She's my main girl, and I don't want to lose her over a mere fling.

Steven, 18

Hmmm. Do these reasons sound familiar? The fact is, both boys and girls answered this question the same way. There's a lot of common sense here (she'd do it if she knew I was doing it) and some kindness (she'd be hurt) and even some long-range thinking (she's the real thing and the other girls are just flings). So, when you think about it, it's not realistic to write a guy off for seeing someone else. There are so many issues involved.

Love matters are always complicated and usually— sooner or later—painful. Nothing is simple when it comes to relationships. Most people spend a lifetime trying to figure out how to behave with the opposite sex, and just when they have it down pat, they're old and wise—too old to get hyper about anything and too wise to let *anyone* drive them crazy. So, enjoy the problems, but don't think they will ever end.

– I KNOW SHE DOESN'T CHEAT ON ME –

Even though boys cheat on you, they don't think you cheat on them. *They are wrong* (as you probably know). Girls cheat on them *plenty*, and then some. (See Chapter 1 of the other half of this book, "What Boys Want To Know About Girls.") Why don't they think you do it? Maybe they can't cope with the idea, or maybe the reasons are more complicated.

She's not the type.

Don, 16

I know she doesn't cheat on me because we are close and we're always together.

Tommy, 17

No, because I trust her and she swore on her mother that she wouldn't.

Jose, 15

I like to think not because it makes my life so much easier.

Pete, 17

Some guys choose to fool themselves into believing that they've got nothing to worry about. Don avoids the doubt by saying: "She's not the type." Tommy rationalizes that it couldn't happen because they are always together, and poor Jose comforts himself with the fact that his girl "swore on her mother." Pete is more honest with himself. He admits that it makes his life easier to believe his girlfriend is faithful. Why play detective only to find information that can hurt you?

I'll bet a lot of guys push thoughts that their girlfriends cheat on them out of their minds. For all their jealousy and suspicion, they really want to believe that you are true to them—even if they know *they* cheat on you.

Part of the reason guys find it easier to believe you don't cheat on them even though they cheat on you is their double standard. Our society has put forth the "Madonna Myth." I'm not talking about the pop singer Madonna. I'm referring to the Madonna in the Bible, the Virgin Mary. Traditionally, women have been expected to live up to the image of the "virgin mother"—pure and faithful, untainted by human desires.

Even though times are changing, and girls are as likely to have more than one sweetheart as guys are, the myth is very much alive. Guys just don't want to believe that girls have needs similar to their own. They prefer to idealize you—to put you high on a pedestal. This sounds wonderful at first. Who wouldn't like to be held in such high esteem? But the problem comes in when they find out that you're really just as human as they are. Perhaps that's why most guys are so unforgiving if they find out you were seeing someone else, yet they expect you to understand if they cheat.

– HAVING YOUR CAKE AND EATING IT, TOO –

I've discovered that the real problem is not the actual cheating, but the fact that most of us want to "have our cake and eat it, too." We wouldn't mind seeing someone other than our boyfriend once in a while, but we don't want our boyfriend to see others. We want it all—the guarantee that our boyfriend will never leave us, but at the same time we want to be free to look around for a "better deal." The only problem is, your boyfriend feels the same way, and more than likely he's doing the same thing you are—going steady (with you) but occasionally "cheating."

Where does all of this leave us? I don't think teenagers who are going out with someone and who see others on the side should be considered to be cheating. I think it should be called "exploring," and what better time than the teen years to explore?

Forgive your boyfriend if you find out he "cheats" on you, but also make an effort to educate him as to why girls also sometimes need to see others. Have your boyfriend read Chapter 1 of the other half of this book, "What Boys Want To Know About Girls." It will help him to cope with a future time when he may find out you cheated on him. (A kind of relationship insurance.) I realize that most guys couldn't cope with this, but perhaps you could even suggest the idea of going steady but seeing other people occasionally.

In the meantime, good luck. I hope you don't break up with your boyfriend just because he went out with someone else. I hope you decide to "live and let live," just the way you would wish him to do if he found out you saw another guy one night.

2

Love, Romance, and Relationships: How Boys Feel

Most girls are very romantic—much more so than boys. This often creates a problem. You wonder what's wrong with him. Why doesn't he think enough of you to send you a dozen roses, or take you for a walk along the lake in the moonlight?

Boys also hold back in the love department. Most girls tell me that guys are reluctant to show emotion. Could it be that they're conditioned to present a cold, hard exterior because of the movie and television image of what a "real man" should be? How can you cope with an unexpressive boyfriend? The answers to these and other questions about the way boys feel about love and romance will be answered in this chapter.

– WHY IS IT SO HARD TO GET A GUY TO SAY "I LOVE YOU"? –

Girls requested that I ask boys the following question: "Why don't you say 'I love you' to a girl if you are going out with her?" Their answers show more than just a fear of not appearing "macho." Listen to this.

> I don't want to get serious about the relationship and I don't want to feel hurt when we break up.
> *Prince, 17*

> She may become so infatuated with me that she'll start calling me all the time and following me around and getting jealous when I talk to other girls.
> *Nelson, 16*

> I don't get too emotional with girls because later they may get out of hand—get too serious. So I'll say something like "I'll always want to be with you."
> *Max, 15*

> If you say it, it makes it that much harder to break up. Then they'd think I never meant it after we break up. They'd believe I was only using them.
> *Jared, 17*

It seems to me that boys are afraid that once they say "I love you" you'll take it more seriously than you should, perhaps reading into it a commitment that isn't there. They're afraid that their own words will trap them into a relationship they're not ready for. Girls, as you know, are about two years ahead of boys emotionally, so you're usually interested in getting "deep" and intense in a relationship before a guy is. But you have to respect the guys for their honesty—even if it means you don't hear what you want to hear.

– HOW DOES A BOY FEEL WHEN YOU TELL HIM YOU LOVE HIM? –

If boys are afraid to tell you they love you, should you hold back your own feelings or say "I love you" if you feel it? Read this and you'll know the answer.

> When she says "I love you" and I don't love her, I feel uncomfortable. I just don't say anything.
> *Tom, 18*

> I feel pressure to say it back, even though I don't feel that way—it makes me nervous.
> *Richie, 16*

> I feel uneasy because I don't want her to be all over me. We are young and I want to finish school and not have love interfere.
> *Joe, 15*

Some guys are not threatened by it, but as you can see (or maybe as you've experienced), most are. They see your declaration of love as pressure on them to make an emotional commitment to you. Play it safe. If you feel that you love a guy, control yourself. Think it and enjoy the feeling, but don't say it. Say instead, "You're terrific. I love being with you." Don't let the thought "If I don't tell him, he may not know" influence you to tell him. Believe me, if you love him, he'll know, and if he feels the same way, he'll eventually speak up. Let him be the one to make declarations of love. It's better to keep a guy worrying "Does she feel the same way I do?" than to have him worrying that you're getting too serious with him.

– HOW DO BOYS FEEL ABOUT ROMANCE? –

Love and romance are not the same. A boy may feel just as strongly about you as you do about him, but his ideas about how to express his feelings tend to be very different from yours. Most guys are not only too embarrassed to be "romantic" (they're afraid of looking foolish) but they wouldn't know how to do it even if they wanted to. Here's what they said when I asked them.

> Right. I'm going to get down on my knees and say, "I beg you your hand in marriage."
>
> *Rob, 16*

> I'd feel like a real ass, arriving at her house with a bunch of flowers in my hand. What if one of my friends saw me?
>
> *Joe, 16*

> It seems like so much work to be romantic. Why can't we just be natural?
>
> *Charlie, 17*

> What am I supposed to do to be romantic? I never really understood what they mean when they say, "Oh, you're so romantic, Johnny."
>
> *Rocko, 15*

Fortunately, some guys are naturally romantic. They say and do all the right things without having to think about it. Others need lessons. For example, if Joe's main problem with giving his girl flowers was not wanting to be seen with them, he could have sent them to her house—the surprise in itself would have been "romantic," and Joe would have avoided the embarrassment of appearing with flowers in his hand. Romance involves the unexpected, the unusual, the exotic. Real romance is far from "corny." It's exciting and adventurous.

Teenage boys often feel embarrassed to give in to their romantic impulses because they're still very concerned about the approval of their male friends. Most guys grow out of this concern as they approach their late teens.

But there is another point you should consider. Some people are just not romantic by nature—they are practical and like everything to be planned and discussed. For example, if you suggest a walk along the beach to a nonromantic guy, he might say something like: "Oh, it's too cold and we'll just get sand in our shoes and sand-flea bites on our legs. Let's stay inside." If you told a guy like that that you love flowers, chances are he'd take you to the flower shop so that you could pick out the flowers you like. He wouldn't want to waste his money on the wrong kind of flowers, and he wouldn't understand if you tried to explain that the whole point was for him to surprise you. He doesn't take chances, and he doesn't see the point of surprises or spontaneous gestures. He's just not romantic.

If you notice these very real nonromantic traits in your boyfriend, maybe you should face the facts: He's not romantic, and he never will be. On the other hand, if you sense romance in your guy but feel he's suppressing it, or just unsure about how to express it, why not get him to read Chapter 2 of the other half of this book: "What Boys Want to Know About Girls." It could help him to dare to yield to his romantic impulses.

– WOULD A GUY CHEAT ON YOU IF YOU WOULDN'T "DO IT"? –

Suppose you have a boyfriend and the two of you are really close. You love him, but you're not having sex with him. Would he go with another girl just for sex? Boys say:

> No. I'm the type of guy who can hold out for a long time.
>
> *Adam, 17*

> Only if I didn't really love my girlfriend. Then of course I would.
>
> *Kenny, 16*

> No. If she likes you, it will happen in due time.
>
> *Walter, 17*

> If she told me she was never going to have sex with me, I might do something.
>
> *Phil, 18*

> No way. I would rather masturbate than go with a sleaze just for sex.
>
> *Joey, 17*

Even boys who might once have gone out with another girl "just for sex" might be less likely to these days, because casual sex is becoming dangerous. As public education about AIDS continues to increase, guys will probably be more and more afraid to take a chance on sleeping with a promiscuous girl.

Guys are capable of using self-control, as you heard from Adam, and if a guy is having trouble holding out, he can always do what Joey does. In any case, it's sad to think that you would make your decision on the basis of fear that he may go out and "do it" with another girl. As Kenny says, a guy would do that only if he didn't really love you in the first place.

– WOULD A GUY BREAK UP WITH YOU IF YOU REFUSED TO HAVE SEX WITH HIM? –

Girls worry that if they keep saying no a guy might break up with them and find another girlfriend who doesn't have such high ideals. Girls, you can set your worries aside. Guys say:

> No, if you really love her; yes, if you don't love her.
>
> *Nick, 17*

> No. Sex is not everything in a relationship.
>
> *Darryl, 17*

> Never. That's immature.
>
> *Charlie, 15*

> No. I respect a girl who says no. It shows that she respects herself.
>
> *Russ, 16*

> Not once in my life did I do that.
>
> *Tom, 18*

Are you surprised? The only guy that would break up with a girl for this reason is one who didn't really care for her in the first place, and, as I'm sure you will agree, the girl is better off without *him*.

– WHY *DO* BOYS BREAK UP WITH GIRLS? –

If they don't leave you because you refuse to have sex with them, why *do* they leave you? I asked boys: "What is the reason you broke up with your last girlfriend?"

We argued too much.
Wilbert, 18

Her parents didn't like me.
Victor, 15

I got tired of her. I saw her every day, and talked on the phone with her every night. We spent too much time together.
Henry, 17

Boredom. She was old news. After a while, a girl gets on your nerves.
John, 17

At first I thought I was in love with her, but after a few weeks she became annoying because she was so intense. I couldn't take her anymore.
Al, 17

She was smothering me. She didn't give me space to breathe.
Robert, 18

Too much of a good thing ruins the joy of it. Think of your favorite dessert. How would you feel about it if you were forced to eat it after every meal? One way to keep your relationship with your boyfriend going is to make yourself scarce. Go out with your friends often. Indulge in shopping sprees with your mother. Visit relatives once in a while, even if at the back of your mind you're thinking: "I wonder if he's meeting new girls?" Let's face it. You can't hold him by being "in his face" all the time.

In certain cases, however, the real problem is not spending too much time together. It's the fact that not every guy and girl are compatible. What once seemed like a relationship made in heaven can turn into a nightmare—in a matter of weeks—when one person starts to notice the different needs he or she has. Al, who complains that his girl was too "intense," probably needed much less from the relationship than his girlfriend did. He broke up with her because he began to feel uncomfortable, not because he hated her or because he was rejecting her as a person.

– WHAT DO GUYS SAY TO THEIR GIRLFRIENDS WHEN THEY WANT TO BREAK UP? –

Did a guy ever break up with you and give you what seemed like a lame excuse for not seeing you anymore? I asked guys: "When you want to break up with a girl, do you tell your girl the truth or do you make up an excuse?"

> It depends on the girl. If you really love her, she deserves to hear the truth.
>
> *Derek, 18*

I tell them the truth: "I just don't like you anymore." The party's over.

Gene, 15

If I found someone else, I'm not going to say, "I found someone else. I don't want to go out with you anymore." I just can't hurt her feelings that way, so I say, "We need some time apart."

Tommy, 17

I usually make up excuses. "I'm not right for you," or something like that.

Steve, 15

When I feel I can't tell the truth, I say, "I need my freedom."

Marty, 18

The true reason can get you in trouble. I'd rather bring up things she did in the past and say something like, "This relationship isn't going anywhere."

Willie, 16

I pick on some little thing she says or does and make a big deal of it—and use it as an excuse.

Carmine, 17

As you can see, some of these brave souls make up excuses, putting the blame on the girl in order to avoid being honest. This is very unfair, because the girl then thinks it is her fault that they're breaking up. She may keep saying to herself, "If only I had done this... if only I hadn't done that," when in fact his reasons for breaking up with her had nothing to do with any failure on her part. Boys often fall out of love—without any good reason—it just happens. Girls do, too, as you may know from your own experience. To put the blame on

- 21 -

someone for something that isn't her fault is a really wimpy thing to do. If your boyfriend did something like this, be glad you're rid of him.

Steve and Marty, who say "We're not right for each other" and "I need my freedom," are much more honest, without being cruelly blunt. They're telling the truth in a kind and considerate way. We could all learn a lesson from these fellows.

Tommy is a diplomat. By saying "We need some time apart," he lets the girl down gently. True, he never intends to go back with her, but he realizes that this method is much kinder than saying something like "I found someone else," which would make most girls feel totally rejected. (Even now I remember with horror the day my boyfriend George came to my house for what I thought was a date and told me he didn't want to see me anymore because he was now going out with Linda, who had, by the way, come *with* him to deliver the message. I locked myself in my room and cried for hours, ashamed to tell even my best friend. It took me a long time to trust boys again.)

– WHY DON'T BOYS CONFIDE IN GIRLS? –

Girls complain that their boyfriends have trouble opening up to them about their dreams and ambitions. Why is this?

> Because they might laugh and tell you you're wasting your time.
>
> *Scott, 16*

> She might think I'm stupid for what I want to be. She may also not be intelligent enough to understand.
>
> *Jared, 17*

She might tease me. And if I don't do it when I get older and go into something else, she may laugh in my face.

Edwin, 15

Boys are more sensitive than we think—they're afraid to take the risk of exposing their innermost thoughts and desires. Only a cruel girl would mock a guy if he told her his dreams and ambitions, no matter how unrealistic they might sound to her. But it seems as if some of these guys have been hurt in just that way. Make sure you're not part of the problem. Communication is hard enough at the best of times. If you put a guy down when he tells you he's going to be a movie star or a millionaire or whatever, the chances are he'll close up the way these boys have.

Boys are reluctant to tell you their problems for the same reason—they're afraid you might make fun of them—and for other reasons, too.

She might not understand.

Andy, 16

Then she would constantly ask you about it and it would be a pain.

Willy, 17

What if she spread it around?

Jack, 15

Sometimes you want to, but you think she might lose respect for you.

Stanley, 18

She might close me out or think I was making things up. I couldn't take the chance.

Rick, 18

Since guys are afraid of being misunderstood or mocked, one of the best ways to make a guy fall in love with you is to become genuinely interested in his problems and then give him lots of encouragement and support. Guys are attracted to girls because of their looks, but they fall in love with them because of their understanding. (See Bibliography for *I Dare You*, for more on this subject.)

– DO GUYS WANT TO GET MARRIED? –

What is the most romantic thing a guy could do for you? He could ask you to marry him. But there's so much talk about guys not wanting to get married. What do the guys have to say for themselves?

> It might feel good to have a wife—when I'm about 25.
>
> *Freddy, 18*

> I want to have a family to jump all over me when I come home from work. I think I'll be ready when I'm 22.
>
> *Jose, 15*

> Yes, I want a son to play with.
>
> *Tommy, 17*

> I'd like to share my life with someone.
>
> *Richie, 16*

> Yes, because I'm in love.
>
> *Nick, 18*

But some boys say:

> No, because it's too much responsibility.
>
> *Jesse, 17*

> I'd rather live my life out. I don't need another mother (wife) to tell me what to do after I leave home.
>
> *Tom, 18*

Most guys want to get married—and for all the right reasons. They look forward to sharing their lives with someone they love, and they want to have children. They're just as concerned about finding the right girl as you are about finding the right guy. But some guys don't want the responsibility or the give-and-take that comes with marriage. Some girls don't, either—which may come as a big surprise to boys who read Chapter 2 of the other half of this book, "What Boys Want to Know About Girls." Jesse and Tom are examples of this type of guy. They may change their minds when they get older, but then again they may not. If they were pushed into marriage, they would make terrible husbands—blaming their wives for their misery. (Remember this for the future. Marry a guy who's even more eager to marry you than you are to marry him.)

A final word about your love life: If your boyfriend makes you cry more than you laugh, GET OUT. Don't walk. Run. He's the wrong guy for you, but there're plenty of others out there to choose from. These are the years for looking over the field. Enjoy them.

3

Arguments: I Say Black—He Says White

No matter how well you get along with your boyfriend, sooner or later, you're going to argue. Many times, boys start the arguments because they're trying to change your behavior.

– NAG, NAG, NAG –

When a guy you're seeing doesn't like something you're doing, he usually lets you know about it. Some guys nag and others just argue. See if any of these themes are familiar to you.

> I complain about how she dresses for work. I don't think she should dress so sloppy.
>
> *Pinto, 15*

> I yell at her when she's nasty to people. I like a girl to have a little class.
>
> *Gary, 18*

I don't want her coming in later than me. She could get in trouble—so I argue about it.
Timmy, 14

Every time I talk to her, she looks around. She doesn't want to miss anything. That gets me mad. I say, "What the hell are you looking at?"
Manuel, 17

"Don't dress that way for work." "Stop being so nasty to people." "I don't want you coming home so late." "Pay attention to me." Doesn't it seem as if such nagging would come from your mother and father rather than from your boyfriend? Who says women are the only ones who nag? Most boys nag because they're concerned that your dress or your behavior will attract other guys, get you into trouble, or bring disgrace upon them. In general, they nag for the same reasons your parents do—because they really care about you. What should you do about their nagging? Immediately hop to it and change your ways? Of course not—but think about what they're saying, and if it makes sense, do something about it. Guys usually have a different perspective on things, and you can often benefit if you think about what they say.

Maybe Pinto's girl is dressing a little too casually for work, and no one would argue that Gary is wrong when he tells his girl not to be nasty to people. But Timmy, on the other hand, may just be jealous about the fact that his girl has a later curfew than he does, and so he tries to hide his jealousy behind concern for her safety.

Other guys pick fights with their girlfriends when they feel they're being treated badly. Such arguments are typical. Manuel's girl is rude to him. By looking around to see who else might be in the room when he's talking, she makes him feel that he isn't important enough to merit her full attention. This would annoy anyone, not just a boyfriend.

What do you do to agitate your boyfriend? Do you mock him in front of people, act dizzy, or laugh loudly in public? If you think you might have been guilty of such behavior, or other actions you're not very proud of, you should listen to his complaints and try to change your behavior the next time the situation arises.

– GETTING THE LAST WORD –

Sometimes guys just argue for the sake of arguing. They like to boss people around—especially girls—and they'll try to bully you with words.

> I'll argue about anything—just to get my point across. I like to have the last word.
>
> *Chris, 15*

> We have different opinions about sex, school, etc. I think I'm right, so I argue.
>
> *Nick, 17*

> Why should I give in to what she says? She thinks she knows it all. I'll just keep insisting that I'm right and she's wrong until she gives up.
>
> *Willie, 16*

> If she wins the argument, then I look bad. I have to keep my image up, you know.
>
> *Gene, 15*

Guys like these have to be right all the time because they have low self-esteem. They see it as a blow to their ego to have to admit that there may be more than one side to an argument. They haven't yet learned that being able to see other people's points of view is a sign of intelligence and maturity—not weakness. Unfortunately, it's almost impossible to have a peaceful relationship with such a fellow. You'll either be forced continually to compromise your own beliefs, pretending to agree with him when you do not, or spend most of your time in heated arguments. This kind of a relationship is not worth the pain. Have a talk with him about his attitude, and if he can't cope with facing himself, let him go—unless you like the aggravation.

– ONE-UPMANSHIP –

Many arguments start because a guy thinks a girl is trying to compete with him. Guys say:

> She talks about how many guys ask her out and she tries to get me jealous.
>
> *Angel, 17*

> We compete about who buys more expensive gifts.
>
> *Roy, 17*

> We argue about who is better looking.
>
> *Fernando, 16*

> She says more guys look at her than girls look at me. I say more girls look at me.
>
> *Sandy, 16*

> We argue about who had better relationships in the past.
>
> *Tan, 17*

> She tries to prove that she's more intelligent than I am—but it's a waste of time. *I am.*
>
> *Lance, 19*

She says her parents are better than mine—my parents have no values, etc., etc.

Val, 15

It's amazing how many issues we've covered here—everything from looks to presents to parents. You'd think people who like each other wouldn't be so competitive. In reality, what seems like competing is actually evaluating. When you start a relationship, you're continually evaluating whether or not he's good enough for you. When Val's girl says her parents are better than his, for example, she's really wondering if he will share her beliefs—her values.

Think of some things you "compete" with your boyfriend about. When you challenge his intelligence, you're really worrying: "Am I falling in love with a guy who's too dumb for me—who's really not on my level?" All of this is normal teenage testing. It's part of finding out who is and who is not right for you. But a lot of it need not be done out loud. That only causes friction and never resolves anything. You don't really think that a discussion of whose parents are better is going to solve anything, do you? So, learn to keep some of these thoughts to yourself. But keep thinking.

– LYING TO AVOID ARGUMENTS –

Some guys claim that they lie to their girlfriends because they know the truth will only cause trouble. See if you think they're right.

I lie if I'm late to avoid a fight, but she usually finds out the lie and we fight, anyway.

Evan, 17

I pretend I'm not interested in looking at other girls, otherwise she would be like a leech and would never trust me when I'm out alone.

Jared, 16

I lie to her about the fact that I smoke reefer because she makes a big deal of it.

Dante, 18

I lie when I hang out with other girls because I don't want to upset her. I know she's jealous.

Steve, 16

I make up a story when I don't show up when I promised so she won't get too upset.

Gus, 19

I lie about hanging out with certain people that she thinks are lowlifes.

Bill, 15

I lie about why I didn't call her. Maybe I just didn't feel like it, but if I tell her that, all hell will break loose.

Victor, 18

I can understand why a guy would lie about being interested in looking at or hanging out with other girls. After all, what is he going to say: "By the way, I was talking to this really hot girl..." You know very well that you don't tell *him* everything (and you shouldn't). But I don't think it's right for guys to lie to you about whether or not they smoke weed or hang out with certain people. You have a right to know what kind of a "character" your boyfriend is. If you catch him in too many lies, realize that it may be just the tip of an iceberg. What else is he hiding? How can you really know a guy if what he tells you about himself is usually a lie? Such relationships are "creepy" because you don't really know who you're with. Sooner or later you'll be in for a surprise—and a painful one at that. If he lies too much, suggest that he get help, and get out before you get hurt. He needs a good psychologist more than he needs a girlfriend.

– ARGUING TO GET THEIR WAY –

Some guys always have to get their own way. Why do they give you such a hard time about where to go on a date, for example? Why can't they just go along with your choice sometimes?

> Girls come up with the most romantic things—which I think are boring.
>
> *Julio, 15*

> If a guy gives in to a girl, she feels she is always going to get her way.
>
> *Boyd, 16*

> Otherwise she might think she has you wrapped around her finger.
>
> *Mark, 17*

> I'm stubborn, and when I don't get my way I get mad.
>
> *Robert, 17*

> They usually want to do something stupid—like see a love movie.
>
> *Rick, 18*

Boys insist on their own way for a variety of reasons. Some are turned off by romantic evenings, some are afraid of losing control, and others are just stubborn. Mature guys, however, are able to compromise and are interested in pleasing *you* once in a while.

> I go where she wants to go. If I make her happy, she'll make me happy.
>
> *Joseph, 17*

> I think you should compromise on what you should do. Agree on something you both enjoy.
> *Hal, 18*

– THE BEST WAY TO AVOID ARGUMENTS –

While some arguments are unavoidable, others can be eliminated by simply attempting to see things from the other person's point of view. If you disagree about something you really care about, instead of just insisting on your own way, which almost never gets you anywhere, say something like: "You have a good point there. I'll think about it; however, will you also give some thought to this idea?"

If you find yourself competing with him—trying to prove that you are better looking, could get more guys than he could get girls, have better parents, and so forth—keep it to yourself. If it's really true, you'll probably leave him soon, anyway. Why make him feel bad about things he can't change? He's probably feeling bad enough about them as it is.

If you think your boyfriend is worth keeping, build up his ego a little instead of constantly putting him down. Give him an honest compliment whenever possible. Tell him how great he is. He probably needs to hear it. (That's why some guys are so busy building themselves up. They haven't gotten enough praise from others.) If you do this, your boyfriend is likely to stop arguing with you so much and start appreciating you more. Try it. It really works. (See Bibliography for *I Dare You*, a book on this and other techniques on how to use psychology to get boys to fall in love with you.)

4

How Do Boys Feel About Spending Time and Money?

Boys like to spend time with girls, of course, but usually not as much time as girls want them to. Why is that? And the same goes for spending money: They enjoy taking a girl out to a movie or buying her a gift once in a while, but not as often as girls expect them to. What do they expect in return for their money? Surprisingly, not what you may be thinking.

This chapter will reveal the reasons why most boys spend more time with their friends than with their girlfriends, yet often expect their girlfriends to sit at home and wait for them. It will also expose the attitudes guys have about spending money on girls. Let's talk about time first.

– WHY DO BOYS EXPECT THEIR GIRLFRIENDS TO SIT AT HOME AND WAIT FOR THEM TO CALL WHILE THEY COME AND GO AS THEY PLEASE? –

When the girls requested that I ask the boys this question, I thought it would be a waste of time. I thought: They'll all deny feeling this way—they'll claim to be perfectly fair and to expect no such thing. But in order to be true to my promise—to make this book a true reflection of what girls really want to know about boys—I asked it. You can imagine my surprise when I found guys admitting:

> When it's me going out, I don't think there's anything wrong, but when she does it I get offended. It's more of an ego trip than anything.
> *Howard, 17*

> If a girl has a boyfriend, she shouldn't go out without him, so if he's hanging out with his friends, she's just going to have to stay home.
> *Manny, 18*

> I expect her to sit home and wait for me if I ask her to. If I tell her I'm going to call at a certain time, I expect her to be there.
> *George, 16*

> Most of us like to hang out with our friends, but we get mad if our girlfriends go out with their friends because we think they may meet other guys—so we try to keep them home.
> *Jack, 17*

> I get annoyed because I'm overprotective.
> *Vincent, 15*

Some nerve. They remind me of Peter in the nursery rhyme. Remember him? He had a wife but couldn't keep her, so cunning Peter put her in a pumpkin shell. "There he kept her very well." Fortunately for girls, things don't work out that way in real life. If a guy wants to be free to go where he pleases, he must allow you the same freedom. Girls today are finding out that it isn't intelligent to let their lives revolve around a guy.

If your boyfriend behaves as any of the above fellows do, and chances are he will if you let him, the best way to set him straight is not to be there when he calls. Then he'll realize that no matter what he says, you are as free as he is. He'll learn he either has to start trusting you or find a robot. And you'll be getting out of the house and doing something more interesting than waiting for the phone to ring.

– WHY DO BOYS SPEND MORE TIME WITH THEIR FRIENDS THAN WITH THEIR GIRLFRIENDS? –

We've already noticed that one of the sources of friction between girls and boys is the time boys spend with their friends at the expense of time that girls think should be spent with them. Whether it's actually more time or not is not the point—girls think it's too much time. Why do boys like to spend so much time with their friends?

> Usually I have a lot more fun with my friends. I have fun with my girlfriend, but it's not the same.

With the guys, you can go out and do things you'd never want the girl to know.

Ryan, 16

You never want to lose your friends, so you keep close ties with them. For instance, if you put too much time into your girlfriend and neglect your friends, more than likely when "breakup time" rolls around, your friends may be reluctant to hang out with you. They'll remember.

Jay, 17

There are only so many things you can do with a girl. For instance, your friends can go play handball with you. Your girlfriend can only go polish her nails.

Tom, 18

You can't take your girlfriend out to get drunk or play football.

Tommy, 17

I don't want to hawk her so much that she gets tired of me or vice versa.

Leigh, 18

Boys say they have more fun with "the guys"—they can do things with them and say things in front of them that they couldn't do or say in front of their girlfriends. It seems as if they need time to be a little wild or crazy—time when they don't have to worry about manners. In short, they need "foolish fun time." Sound immature? Well, as a matter of fact, most girls are two years ahead of guys emotionally. Girls have grown out of the need to hang out with girls so much and are now looking to build deep, emotional relationships with the opposite sex.

But even if a girl goes out with a guy two years older than she is, she may still find that he wants to spend more time with his friends than she likes. Why? From elementary school on, boys are encouraged to participate in team sports. They learn early in life to develop a camaraderie—a "horsing around with the boys" attitude. As boys mature, they retain their need for this "masculine fellowship."

Although team sports exist for girls, too, they are not as important. In high school, girls are encouraged to be cheerleaders. Get the picture? A girl is taught, indirectly, that her function is to get behind a guy and "cheer him on." I always resented this idea and wondered why they didn't have a bunch of guy cheerleaders for *girls'* team sports.

Things are changing, and girls are being encouraged to be less dependent on guys, but as it stands, girls still tend to demand more time with their boyfriends than boys are willing to give.

How can you make peace with the situation? Reeducate yourself. This is one time you could learn something from the boys. Realize that you don't have to spend every waking moment with your boyfriend. Learn to value the time you spend with your girlfriends. They're not just second best. And as Jay points out, it's your friends who will be there for you when you break up with your current love—but only if you've kept in touch with them.

The other thing you can do with the time you don't spend with your boyfriend is to engage in all sorts of sports and activities. You can join a gym and work out, for instance. You won't lose anything when it comes to your relationship with your boyfriend. In fact, you'll gain something because you'll be giving each other space to be yourselves. In addition, you'll be gaining something from whatever activity you've chosen to participate in. If you join a gym, you'll be gaining the self-confidence that comes from improving your body and the high that comes from exercise. If this interests you, see the bibliography for a weight-training book.

– WHAT GUYS WANT IN RETURN FOR THEIR MONEY –

Time isn't the only thing you and your boyfriend may argue about. How to spend money is the other big one. Boys tend to be just as definite about how they want to spend their money as they are about how they spend their time. And as you might expect, they definitely want something in exchange for their money. But what that something is may come as a surprise to you. Here's what they said when asked if they wanted anything in return for a gift or a special night out.

> Yes, I do. I expect respect for the things I buy her. I don't expect sex because I don't have to buy something for a girl to get it. I'll just get a slut.
> *Rob, 16*

> When I spend money on a girl I expect her to appreciate it and just say thanks. That's the polite thing to do. A girl shouldn't take advantage of a guy who is being a gentleman.
> *Jerome, 16*

> If I spend my hard-earned money on a girl, I'm showing her I care for her, and all I expect in return is that she show me she appreciates it.
> *Doogle, 18*

> When I spend money on a girl I'm hoping that she will love me.
> *Harry, 19*

> I enjoy spending money on my girlfriend because she appreciates it.
>
> *Luis, 17*

What do boys want? Appreciation. When your boyfriend takes you out and spends money on a movie and refreshments, do you just take it for granted or do you let him know you appreciate it? Guys don't resent spending money on you, but they do resent it when you don't even acknowledge that they did it. It's so easy to do. All you have to do is say "Thank you."

– HOW DO GUYS FEEL ABOUT ACCEPTING GIFTS FROM GIRLS? –

Should you do more than thank him? Should you spend money on him or buy him gifts? Would this make a guy feel uncomfortable? It depends.

> I feel happy when a girl gives me a gift—but if it's too expensive, I won't take it.
>
> *Paulie, 17*

> I feel good because someone likes me enough to give me something.
>
> *Darryl, 16*

> I love it when a girl gives me gifts. It shows me that she's thinking about me and doesn't only want *me* to spend money on her.
>
> *Cliffy, 17*

> I don't mind, but sometimes I feel that they expect something in return, whether it's a gift or a date.
>
> *David, 16*

> I hate receiving gifts from girls. I'm embarrassed and I don't know what to say. I'd rather give the presents than receive them.
>
> *Timmy, 18*

Most guys appreciate a surprise gift, but you've got to be careful not to make them feel uncomfortable. A very expensive gift will embarrass a guy. He'll think, "This makes me look cheap. I should be buying her..." or "Now I'm obligated to do the same..." or "This must mean she's getting too serious about me. I'd better cool this relationship." So it seems like the best thing to do is give something that is more thoughtful than it is expensive. Select something that shows you appreciate his unique personality. Be creative.

A good way to show appreciation for a guy is to offer to take him out to dinner for a special occasion or to pick up the tab for a movie and refreshments once in a while. I don't encourage girls to do this too often because it's easy for a guy to "get spoiled." I'm from the old school. I would be very turned off by a guy who expected me to "split the bill" every time. Ugh. How unromantic. If he can't afford it, I'd rather go to the local pizza place and let him pay the full bill than go to a fancy restaurant where I have to split the bill. Except for special circumstances, guys should pay, and most of them still do without complaint. If you feel otherwise, there's nothing wrong with it—as long as it doesn't bother you.

The secret to a happy relationship with your boyfriend when it comes to spending time and money is give-and-take. Can you give each other the "space" each of you needs? Do you respect each other's feelings about spending money, even if you don't agree with them? If the answer to either of these questions is no, you two are headed for trouble.

Time and money issues are crucial in all marriages and can even lead to divorce. It's your job, as a teenager, to look into your feelings about these things and to be honest with yourself about your needs. If you do this now, you may break up with a boyfriend or two, but it's much better than breaking up your marriage later, when you discover that you now hate the fabulous man you married because he thinks a new car every year is the most important thing in the world and you think that money should be going into savings, or vice versa.

5
How Boys Really Feel About Sex

Why do boys try their best to get a girl into bed, yet claim they want to marry a virgin? Why do guys think it's wonderful if they have sex with anyone they can get into bed, yet look down on girls who do the same? What are some of the favorite lines guys use to try to get a girl into bed? Can guys control themselves—do they *have* to have sex? All of these issues, and more, will be discussed in this chapter.

– IF A GIRL DOES IT, IT'S CHEAP –

When it comes to sex, most guys have a double standard. They don't respect a girl who has sex with lots of guys, but they think sleeping around is what guys are supposed to do. Why?

It just doesn't seem right. Girls who have sex with lots of guys are sluts.

Jeff, 16

Girls are supposed to have more self-respect than guys. When a guy has a lot of girls it's macho. When a girl does it—it's cheap.

Chris, 15

She should have more common sense.

Scott, 16

If a guy has sex a lot of his friends congratulate him and he's a stud. If a girl does it, it's cheap.

Tom, 18

It's the guy's place to try to have sex with a girl—and it's the girl's place to turn him down. The girls who don't are "easy" and become known as freaks.

Ronnie, 16

The girl is giving up something—we aren't. To us it's a conquest, a dare.

Leigh, 17

Girls like that get a reputation and some of us wouldn't even go with them because of it.

Fernando, 16

As mentioned on p. 44, boys have higher standards for girls than they do for themselves. They expect girls to "know better," to have more self-control and more self-respect. And although what they've told us here is what we already know—that girls get a bad reputation for the same behavior that earns boys a good reputation—the fact remains that even if they can't explain why this is so, it *is*. It is not fair, but it is a fact.

– WHAT GOES THROUGH A GUY'S MIND WHEN HE TRIES TO SEDUCE A GIRL HE BARELY KNOWS? –

> Why not?
>
> *John, 15*

> Sometimes I just want to have cheap sex and not be bothered afterwards.
>
> *Lonnie, 18*

> I just want to see how many different girls I can have sex with.
>
> *Mike, 16*

> I think the girl has a great body and she would be good in bed. It's as simple as that.
>
> *Gene, 17*

> Some girls give you the impression that they would be willing, so I always figure, why not try?
>
> *Johnny, 17*

These guys were a lot more honest with me than they're likely to be when they're trying to get *you* into bed. You can see why your parents warn you that guys who try to get you into bed are out for "one thing only." Often they are.

– IF SHE HAD SEX WITH ME, SHE MUST HAVE DONE IT WITH LOTS OF GUYS –

Girls often sleep with guys as a means of holding on to them, but this can backfire. Sleeping with someone can make him drop you cold after the novelty of sex wears off. It's not fair, but it's true. Girls want to know: "Why do you leave a girl once you have sex with her? How do you think a girl feels when you do something like that?"

> When a guy has sex with a girl he just met, he leaves her because who wants to get serious with a slut?
>
> *Don, 18*

> Guys use girls. Girls feel hurt and disrespected, but boys don't care because they weren't looking to have a relationship—just a one-night stand.
>
> *Scott, 16*

> She's just another screw. I was horny. I don't love her.
>
> *Carl, 15*

> Some guys think it's cool. They don't realize the girl might be looking for love and may want to stay with them.
>
> *Jared, 16*

> That's something I've only done to girls I don't care about. I guess it must make a girl say to herself: I should never have done that.
>
> *Tony, 17*

> I say to myself, "If she had sex with me, she must have had sex with lots of other guys," and that really turns me off.
>
> *Jose, 15*

Guys want their girl to be special—not someone who goes to bed with lots of guys. Which brings me to another of the questions you girls wanted me to ask the boys—and one with some surprising answers.

– DOES VIRGINITY STILL MATTER? –

If I am ever going to marry, it must be to a virgin. I don't want to live with someone for the rest of my life knowing she has had sex with other men. A girl who stays a virgin until she is married is my kind of wife.

Tom, 18

Yes—because you know she doesn't have any diseases.

Scott, 16

I would love to marry a virgin. As a matter of fact, my girl is a virgin and I have a lot of respect for her. I have future plans for us.

Michael, 17

If she is untouched, then no one could ever say: "I had sex with his wife."

Jo-Jo, 14

Definitely. For a girl to save her virginity for her husband—she has to be pretty special. It will make me love her more.

Tommy, 17

Of course I would. That way she would be fresh out of the pack, pure and tender.

Dom, 18

Yes. A girl becomes infatuated with the first guy she makes love to. She would always be mine.
Aron, 17

At least you know sex meant something to her.
Jared, 17

– WHY DO GUYS TRY TO PRESSURE GIRLS INTO HAVING SEX? –

If guys want to marry virgins, it doesn't seem fair that they try so hard to convince girls to have sex with them. And it isn't—but they do it, anyway. Why? This was one of the questions girls most wanted me to ask the guys. Here's what they answered.

Because I'm horny.
Charlie, 15

If I don't, I may never get anything!
Andy, 16

I don't pressure them—I just persuade them in my own way.
Anthony, 17

After a guy is going out with a girl for a while, he usually gets impatient and starts to pressure her. It's just hard to resist.
Jamal, 18

As you can see, the answer is pretty simple. They try to get girls into bed because they want to. They're not thinking about anything except what *they* want. What they want is determined by their sex drive, which is much higher than a girl's sex drive. This becomes especially apparent to girls who have slept with their boyfriends. They complain that their boyfriends are never satisfied. "He's always after me," they say, "whether I want to or not. Why?"

Most guys are always in the mood.
Stewart, 16

A guy feels that when he's in the mood, there's no stopping him. Whether or not she's up for it, it doesn't matter.
Mack, 18

If you wait until she's in the mood, you may wait forever.
Peter, 17

Girls will usually give in—after a little coaxing.
Jimmy, 19

On a scale of one to ten, a teenage boy's sex drive is somewhere between eight and ten—it's at its peak. But a teenage girl's sex drive is just beginning to be awakened. Her sex drive is somewhere between one and two. Women reach their sexual peak in their thirties. No wonder guys have to do a lot of pressuring and convincing to get a girl into bed. Boys are literally "driven" by their hormones, while girls find it much easier to control themselves because their sex drive is still comparatively slight.

– LINES GUYS USE TO GET GIRLS INTO BED –

In their effort to apply pressure, guys resort to "lines." Do any of the following sound familiar?

Trust me. I'm different.
Nick, 18

You know what true love is, baby—and this is it.
Eddie, 17

I really care for you. I would never leave you.
Paul, 16

"Let's go in the other room," as I pull her gently by the arm.
Anthony, 17

We've been going out for a while. Are you ready to go all the way yet?
Jeff, 17

It isn't what I say—it's the way I act. I start kissing her and then things happen.
Tom, 18

You're the most beautiful thing on earth. I will always respect you.
Charlie, 15

Baby, I know you want me—so why don't you let me make your fantasies come true?
Ray, 18

You might want to let the guy know that you're familiar with his line—and are not going to fall for it, even if you've fallen for him.

– DO GUYS LIE TO GET YOU INTO BED? –

Guys use lines, but how far would a guy go to convince a girl to go to bed with him? Would he lie and say he loves a girl just to get her into bed?

> I once lied to a girl and told her I felt a lot for her. All I wanted was sex. I regretted it because after that she was hurt.
>
> *George, 18*

> I told this girl I loved her and that if she had sex with me I would love her more. I just said it to get her into bed.
>
> *Joe, 17*

> No, I don't because love is a meaningful word and I don't have to lie to get sex.
>
> *Darryl, 17*

> Yes, because she was hot and she had the nicest body. I don't regret it at all.
>
> *Lennie, 17*

> I just might say I like them a lot—not I love them. It's their decision. I try to talk them into it.
>
> *Oscar, 16*

Some would lie about loving you, and others wouldn't. I don't think your decision about whether or not to have sex with a guy should be based on whether or not he says he loves you. You can become far too emotionally involved with a guy when you have a sexual relationship with him. It's much easier to cope with a breakup if you haven't had sex with a guy. I'm convinced that girls who try to kill themselves over broken love affairs are the ones who got sexually involved. Girls' hearts tend to follow the lead of their bodies. This makes them very vulnerable to guys, who, as you've just read, have no trouble keeping sexual feelings separate from emotions.

As a young person, you should save your emotional and mental energy for other teenage problems—finishing school, making career decisions, etc. A sexual involvement at this time can actually change your destiny—ruin your entire life. Practice saying the word no.

– WHY DO GIRLS SAY YES? –

I put this question here instead of in the boys' section of the book because boys don't wonder why. They're just glad when a girl does it. But girls do wonder. Often, even girls who have had sex aren't clear about why they did it. I think that most girls say yes because they want to feel closer to their boyfriends—they like being held and cuddled. A girl also enjoys the power she feels over the guy at that most intimate moment when she knows that she alone is the cause of his pleasure. Some girls get a feeling of love at this moment, and girls who are lacking in love because of unhappy family situations are in danger of becoming addicted to sexual experiences as a replacement for the love that is missing from their home lives.

Why do other girls, who *are* loved at home and who seem secure, give in to their boyfriends, even though they don't really want to have sex with them? Many girls do it, believe it or not, as a favor to their boyfriends. They sense their boyfriends' needs and they feel as if they should satisfy those needs. I don't think this is a good idea, ladies. You should perform your works of charity outside of the bedroom.

– IS IT PHYSICALLY POSSIBLE FOR GUYS TO CONTROL THEMSELVES WHEN THEY ARE SEXUALLY AROUSED? –

Girls have heard so many things about guys' sexuality. "Don't get him too excited. He won't be able to control himself and then he may rape you." Is it true? Are guys like uncontrollable animals when they become aroused, or do they, in fact, have the ability to use restraint? Here's what guys say.

> Personally, I can control myself. Not having sex helps me to build up my inner strength, confidence, etc.
>
> *Donald, 17*

> Yes, I can. The best form of birth control is self-control.
>
> *Frank, 15*

> If you love a girl, you can control yourself, even though it's difficult.
>
> *Frisco, 18*

> I'm not desperate. If you are talking to a girl, you don't have to let sex take over your mind.
>
> *Albert, 16*

> I guess you don't really *have* to have sex. It's nice to get lucky once in a while. It's much better than masturbating.
>
> *Willie, 17*

Guys are not animals—they can control themselves (no matter what they say at the time about not being able to). But remember, you should never let a guy force you to do anything you don't want to do. Your needs are just as important as his. And you have the right—and the power—to exert your own will.

A lot of girls think that if they go too far, they have to go all the way because there's some "point of no return" in making out. Surprisingly enough, guys themselves don't see it this way.

> When we're making out, I have a quick physical reaction and then I don't know what to do with myself, so I want to make one of those love scenes. But if a girl says no, I figure that's her right.
>
> *Clay, 18*

> Some guys blame the girl. They think she tried to get him all hot and horny and just tease him, but that's not true. Guys just get that way.
>
> *Billy, 16*

> I don't always assume it has to lead to something, but I can hope, can't I?
>
> *Luke, 17*

– AS OLD-FASHIONED AS IT MAY SEEM –

Sure they can hope, but let them know you're hoping to save yourself for your husband. As old-fashioned as it may seem, I say wait until you're married. It's much easier for you to wait than it is for a guy because your sex drive is much less intense. All you have to do is keep saying no.

Sex is not supposed to be just for pleasure. It should be part of a deep, lasting relationship. But even if you don't care about that, it's dangerous to be promiscuous these days. There's safety and self-respect in self-control. Marriage is in again. People are returning to the idea of having sex with only one partner—their spouse. Those people are in no danger of getting AIDS.

Can you wait? Guess what! No one ever died from *not* having sex. *But people did die from having it*. Think about that for a moment.

– WHAT IF YOU'VE ALREADY HAD SEX? –

What if you've already had sex? Does that mean you have to continue to have sex with the next boyfriend and the next and so on? Of course not. Guys may try to pressure you by saying "I know you had sex with him, so you have to have sex with me." But they don't *know*. In fact, guys lie to each other all the time about their sexual experiences, and all of them know that they do. So you can say you're a virgin, no matter what your former boyfriend is going around saying. Can anyone prove you're not? No. Not even a doctor can be one-hundred-percent sure. If you want to, you can wait until you're married before you have sex again. Then when you get married, you'll feel like a virgin—even if, technically speaking, you're not. As a matter of fact, I don't recommend that you say you're not a virgin if anybody asks. Your sexual history is your own business.

6

I Can Never Figure Out Why Boys... (Strange Ways of Boys)

There are certain things about boys that are puzzling to most girls. Why do guys act differently toward you when they're around their friends? Why do they get so furious when you don't respond to their flirting? Why do they try to rule you? Why all the questions about your past? Why do they tease you about your hair, shape, makeup, etc.? In this chapter, you'll find out why boys behave the way they do toward girls.

– "WE HAVE TO BE MR. MACHO MAN IN FRONT OF OUR FRIENDS" –

Most boys put on a different "face" when they're with their friends. Girls complain that their boyfriends don't even seem like the same person when they're around their friends. Why do boys act one way when they're alone with their girlfriends and another way when they're in a crowd?

> When I'm alone with my girl I show sensitivity toward her, but when my friends are around I have to act masculine—to prove to my friends that I have the upper hand. When they're not around it doesn't go that way, of course.
>
> *John, 18*

> Sometimes when I'm with my girl and my friends I try to be bossy, but it doesn't work. When my girl and I are alone I'm the most romantic, lovable person in the world.
>
> *Rob, 17*

> I act different because I wouldn't want my friends to know she means the world to me. When they're around I don't pay much attention to her.
>
> *Joel, 16*

> We have to be cool when we're in front of our friends—like Mr. Macho Man.
>
> *Rodney, 15*

> I feel I have to impress them—so I laugh loud and act weird, but when we're alone I can be myself.
>
> *Evan, 17*

Guys are ashamed to let their friends know that they have deep feelings for a girl. They want to maintain a tough "macho" image. The funny thing is, all the guys are putting on the same act. They all act tough and indifferent in front of their friends, but, as they admit, they take off the mask and act sensitive and caring as soon as they're alone with their girlfriends.

Don't let it bother you. By the time a guy reaches his twenties, he's not ashamed to be himself with you—even if his friends are around. In the meantime you'll just have to be patient.

– WHY DO GUYS TURN MEAN IF YOU REFUSE TO TALK TO THEM? –

When a guy tries to flirt with a girl, she takes a long, hard look at him and decides whether or not she likes him. If she doesn't, she usually lets him know by body language. She'll put her chin in the air, refuse to smile, or just walk away without answering. She thinks that's an acceptable response. Guys take it as an insult. Here's why.

> There's no need to turn your head up to the sky and switch away just because I said hi. I mean, it's just common courtesy to at least say hello when someone says it to you.
>
> *Leigh, 18*

> I hate it when a girl you're trying to talk to gives you a snotty attitude and acts like she's above you.
>
> *Keith, 15*

> Why does she think she can't talk to me? If a girl went up to me, I would talk to her, ugly or not.
>
> *Nando, 17*

> A guy feels rejected when a girl ignores him, so to make himself look good he feels he has to rank the girl out.
>
> *Jeff, 17*

A guy feels stupid when a girl doesn't want to go out with him.

Scott, 16

Boys (and men also, for that matter) are very sensitive about being rejected when they approach a woman. Try to be kind. After all, it's a compliment when a guy is attracted to you—even if he's not your type. Have a heart when you're letting a guy know you're not interested. Think how hard it would be if girls had to make the first move. You'd hope guys you'd approach would at least let you down gently.

So if a guy you don't care for says hello with the goal of flirting with you, give him a friendly "Hi" back. You can let him know you're not interested in a romantic relationship by the way you say it. Just be very pleasant but businesslike and keep moving as fast as you can. He'll get the message, yet his ego will be spared.

– WHY ARE GUYS AFRAID TO APPROACH A GIRL THEY'RE REALLY ATTRACTED TO? –

For the same reasons discussed previously, guys will often refuse to talk to the girl they're attracted to. Their fear of rejection often causes them to miss out on meeting the girl they really want to meet.

> I'm afraid she'll reject me. It would ruin my macho act. If I get turned down, then when I go to school everyone will know about it.
>
> *Michael, 17*

> I want to go out with someone I'm superior to. I'd rather be the better-looking one. If I'm not, then

she may be looking for other guys. This way, she'll be clinging to me.

Dave, 16

I think she may already have a boyfriend.

Chris, 15

I want the girls to come to me. I never make the first move.

Paulie, 18

Their fragile egos won't allow them to risk being turned down, even if it's for a legitimate reason such as a girl having a boyfriend. They picture everyone in school finding out that they were rejected and they imagine a large audience of mockers laughing at them. For this reason, many guys choose to play it safe. They either approach girls who are obviously not as good-looking as they are or they take no chances at all. Like Paulie, they simply refuse to make the first move.

You can use this information to your advantage. If you like a guy who seems to be afraid to approach you, why not make the first move? It's really not that difficult. Just go up to him and ask him a question about something. For example, if you're on the beach, you can ask him for the time or when the last bus is leaving, etc. You could also give a guy a compliment. Sticking with the beach example, you could compliment his tan, his bathing suit, or even his muscles. Right now you may be saying: "No way. I'd look like a fool." But that isn't true at all. If you think about what we've just discussed—how guys, no matter how good-looking they are, are unsure of their ability to attract girls—you will realize that any guy would more than appreciate a compliment. Even if the guy doesn't end up going out with you, he'll love you for the moment because you helped to build up his self-confidence.

So the next time you see a guy you want to meet and that guy is talking to every girl except you, make the first move. You've got nothing to lose and everything to gain.

– WHY DO GUYS ACT SO BOSSY? –

Guys feel obliged to live up to the image of boss and protector. For this reason, they sometimes go a little overboard and attempt to dominate you. Listen to some of these he-men. Actually, some of them sound like cavemen to me, though some girls may still like this kind of behavior.

> I have to be overprotective, because there are a bunch of———s out in the streets. I have to watch out for her.
>
> *Jose, 15*

> I want her to be mine and only mine. I have to be in control or I'll look like a wimp. That's just the way it is.
>
> *Todd, 17*

> I always look after my investments.
>
> *Larry, 18*

> The guy should always be in control—otherwise there will be trouble. I'm a little old-fashioned.
>
> *Tom, 18*

> I have to show her who's boss. If I'm not in control I feel inferior.
>
> *Jason, 16*

If you don't they will take advantage of you and treat you like a sucker. She'll think you're soft.
Red, 17

I'm a man. We have our pride. A man is supposed to be strong and in control.
Stanley, 16

If I don't, she may control *me*.
Ron, 17

In my house and on TV men rule women. That's the way it is.
David, 16

Most girls like guys who are willing and able to protect them, but they don't appreciate being bossed around. The world is changing, and this generation of teenage boys is struggling to find their proper role in it. Try to be patient. Guys are having a hard time learning where to draw the line. They sense that we don't respect a wimp, yet they see that we become furious when they try to dominate us. If you are clear about where *you* want the line drawn, while still being affectionate with him when he steps over it, he'll get the message; but at the same time, because of your loving attitude, he won't be able to get too angry about it.

– WHY DO GUYS WANT TO KNOW ABOUT THEIR GIRLFRIENDS' OLD BOYFRIENDS? –

Did you ever notice that most guys you go out with ask lots of questions about your past life? Here's why they do it and what you should say in response.

I want to know what I'm getting involved in. It wouldn't be cool to go to another town and hear people say, "Oh, she's a slut."

Pete, 16

She might have been a floozie. I don't want people to laugh at me behind my back when I walk down the street with her.

Bill, 18

I don't want to get serious with her, then find out she put out for the town.

Eric, 18

It helps me to figure out her personality.

Joe, 16

So you can be ready for her in the future—is she a freak, will she try to use you?

Freddy, 15

Guys always like to know who the girl went out with and what she did with the guy and if she was happy, etc.

Jerry, 17

It's just conversation.

Donald, 16

So I don't make the same mistakes her past boyfriends made.

Nick, 17

I want to know what she's been through.

George, 17

It's normal for two people to ask each other lots of questions about their backgrounds and experiences when they first meet. It's really the only way to get to know a person. If you feel, however, that a guy is grilling you about your past to dig up information regarding your sexual activities, I don't blame you for being insulted. A guy should have more sensitivity than that, and if he doesn't, don't hesitate to put him in his place. You don't have to tell him anything you don't want to. In fact, my advice is, keep your past to yourself. If you talk too much, you'll only get yourself in trouble. Certain things should be left a mystery. Let him keep wondering.

– WHY DO GUYS TEASE GIRLS? –

You would think guys would realize by now that no girl appreciates being teased about her personal appearance —yet most teenage boys continue to laugh and joke about your hair, makeup, shape, and clothing, even if they're attracted to you. In fact, sometimes the more they like you, the more they tease you. Why?

> That's the way you get to meet a girl—you tease her about her hair or something.
> *Alex, 16*

> I do it because they're always worrying about their hair and makeup. Boys don't wear makeup so I guess we find it interesting and we tease.
> *Mike, 16*

> Sometimes girls overdo the makeup and destroy their natural beauty. They need to be told.
> *Lance, 18*

> Guys just love to pick on girls. I think that's how a guy shows he likes her. He gives her attention, but he does it the wrong way.
> *Don, 18*

> Sometimes I do it to be a pest. Other times I do it to get back at her for being a pain in the ass to me.
> *Dean, 14*

> Because girls have heart attacks if they don't think they look perfect. It's funny.
> *Frank, 15*

Obviously, boys use teasing as a means to get your attention. Believe it or not, it's their lame way of flirting with you. I've told them that they should compliment you instead (in Chapter 6 of the other half of this book, "What Boys Want to Know About Girls"). But I don't think most boys will change overnight just because I tell them to. As they become more mature, they'll learn how women like to be treated. For now, just say to yourself, "Boys will be boys," and try not to take it personally. Notice that most of the boys don't mean to be cruel. They do it to get your attention, to be funny, or just to see how you'll react. So if it bothers you, don't react. That'll really stop the teasing.

As a general rule, if you want to save yourself unnecessary emotional turmoil the next time your boyfriend, or any boy for that matter, does something that hurts, annoys, or offends you, before you get angry, ask yourself: "What is really going on here? Is he trying to save face in front of his friends? Is he just trying to flirt with me? Does he think I'm rejecting him?" Once you think about what's going on under the surface, you'll find that often you can not only act cool, but *be* cool. It's great when you feel in control of your own emotions and know that nobody can get to you with childish insults. Save your emotions for the things that matter.

7

What Turns a Guy Off? What Turns a Guy On?

Do you sometimes wonder why you can't seem to get the guys you like to ask you out? Maybe there's something you're doing or saying or even wearing that turns guys off. The guys I interviewed had plenty to say on that subject.

And once you've heard what turns them off, you'll want to know what traits and mannerisms really turn them on. What do guys love in a girl?

In this chapter, guys tell it all. Find out what you've been doing right and what you've been doing wrong, and learn what you have to do to get the guy you want to fall in love with you.

– BEHAVIOR TURN-OFFS –

Certain behavior causes guys to run the other way, and what they say about behavior they don't like shows they have a lot of common sense.

Girls who smoke everyday and are not interested in anything but getting high turn *me* off. I picture myself introducing her to my mother. Hi, Ma. I'd like you to meet Rosey. And Rosey has this dazed look in her eyes.

Joe, 15

I hate showoffs who hang all over guys. It's as if they're putting on a big act to get guys to think they're wild or older than they are. I appreciate girls who just act natural.

Jerry, 17

If a girl is stuck-up or snotty or self-centered, stay away from me. I don't need anybody who acts like they'd be doing me a favor if they go out with me.

Gemel, 14

Bad manners. I have a taste for etiquette. It disgusts me when a girl cracks gum in your face, talks with food in her mouth, or shoves her way in front of a line. That's not my idea of a lady.

Howard, 17

Getting high is out of style. These days, too much is known about the effect of drugs (even marijuana) on the mind—not to mention the body. Guys reject girls who do drugs. They look at them as lowlifes.

Guys hate girls who seem to be stuck-up, who act as if they think they're too good for them. Girls often behave this way without even realizing that it might be offensive. They think they're *supposed* to act aloof. It's a defense many girls use to protect themselves against possible rejection. The only trouble is, boys don't know this. If you put on airs in front of a guy you really like, he may take you seriously and reject you because he really believes you think you're too good for him.

If you like a guy, play it straight and be yourself. Be warm and friendly. That's the best way to get him—not by acting cold and stuck-up.

Guys expect girls to have good manners, regardless of what kind of manners they have. They look at good manners as a feminine trait. If you're loud, rude, crude, and inconsiderate, most boys will run, even the ones who often act the exact same way. Just because he does it doesn't mean he thinks it's okay for you to do it. So don't try to win points with a guy by imitating his crude behavior. In fact, he may end up giving up his bad manners if you embarrass him into it with your good ones.

– FASHION TURN-OFFS –

This category includes clothing as well as grooming. If you want a guy to head for the hills, do what any of the girls described below are doing.

> I can't stand girls who dress slutty—tight, cheap, mismatched clothes with their bodies hanging out all over the place. They look as if they're trying to imitate prostitutes on Forty-second Street. What do they think, that turns a guy on?
>
> *Tony, 16*

> A girl who doesn't shave her legs or her armpits disgusts me. No matter how pretty she is, I can't help picturing myself touching her or kissing her and it just grosses me out.
>
> *Bob, 17*

> If I meet a girl with bad breath, I run. I mean, you can't even stand next to her, and who would want to get close enough to kiss her. It also makes you think she's dirty, even if she's neat and clean.
>
> *Steve, 16*

Most guys are not concerned with high fashion, but they don't like "cheap." They appreciate a girl who dresses in good taste. Some girls think they impress guys and look sexy when they wear their clothing too tight, but instead of impressing guys, they often end up disgusting them.

I recognize myself—when I was a teenager. I was very thin and rather underdeveloped for my age, so I thought I would make it up by wearing what I thought were sexy clothes. I "pegged" my skirt so tight I could hardly walk in it. I really thought I looked great, and I guess I believed that all the boys would suddenly go for me. But, lucky for me, my parents caught me every time I tried to leave the house with such an outfit on and made me change. They would say: "Joyce, you are making the wrong statement about yourself when you dress like that. It's not the way to impress a guy." At the time I didn't appreciate their interference, but as the years went by, everything I learned about men confirmed their statements. Guys are not impressed with girls who are "obvious" in their attempt to look sexy. They admire girls who are more subtle in their dress style.

Basic grooming is a must. You may not think guys notice, but they do. Guys can't stand to see body hair on a girl. Of course, they may not tell the girl that, but they usually eliminate her as a possible date as soon as they notice it, even if they like everything else about her.

You can imagine how bad breath or body odor would turn anyone off. Since this is so obvious, I don't think girls who are guilty of these turn-offs are aware that they have a problem. If they did, they'd use mouthwash or deodorant, or bathe more frequently—whatever it takes. This means you should check yourself. Maybe you *are* one of these girls and you don't even know it, or maybe one of your friends has this problem. If you tell her, you'll be doing her a *big* favor. Many people go through life being rejected because of such problems,

- 70 -

just because people are too embarrassed to tell them what's wrong.

– VERBAL TURN-OFFS –

I think a lot of girls believe that guys are impressed if they talk real tough or sophisticated. But the ones I've heard from all agree they can't stand:

> Bad-mouthed girls who talk like truck drivers. I hate that. It's embarrassing to me. I actually cringe when every other word out of a girl's mouth is f——ing this and f——ing that.
>
> *Carl, 15*

> Girls that talk about their past sexual experiences turn me off. I start picturing the details of what they did with these other guys and I say to myself, "Someday she'll be talking about what I did with her."
>
> *Tom, 18*

> I can't stand to hear girls tell dirty jokes. I try to pretend it's okay, but I really feel very uncomfortable. It just doesn't seem right. I could just picture myself out on a date with my girl and she starts telling these raunchy jokes. How does that make *me* look?
>
> *Rick, 17*

Guys are not interested in girls who can keep up with them when it comes to cursing. They think it's okay for *them* to curse and be crude, and they usually do when they're with "the boys" (that's how the phrase "locker-room talk" came into being), but if you try to join them, their reaction is: "What a lowlife." They especially don't like it if you use bad language in front of their friends.

Guys feel very threatened when girls go into details about their sexual experiences. That's a fast way to lose their respect. As you already know, most guys have a double standard when it comes to sex. They don't appreciate a girl who's "been around," much less one who brags about it. So don't get tricked into talking. They may ask questions, but that doesn't mean they really want the answers.

Guys also hate for girls to tell dirty jokes. They may laugh when a girl does this—they don't want to look like prudes—but they're really uncomfortable about it. They'd rather you leave the dirty jokes to them.

Do you know anyone who is guilty of any of the above "turn-offs"? If *you* are, don't feel too bad. Just take action immediately. Correct your fault and then forget it. Be glad you were able to catch the problem early in life. Some women who are well past the teen years are still guilty of some of the above "turn-offs." I'll bet you can think of a few you've met in your lifetime.

Let's move to the positive half of this chapter—what turns guys on. As you might expect, guys are just as definite about what they love as about what they hate.

– BEHAVIOR TURN-ONS –

Guys appreciate simplicity and kindness in a girl. They enjoy girls who behave:

> Like a lady—polite and loving. She should be caring and helpful.
>
> *Joe, 15*

> Relaxed. She should give me space but still show that she's concerned with what I'm doing.
>
> *Erik, 16*

She should be sensitive to my feelings and she should tell me how she feels.

Gary, 17

I love a girl who gets along with her family and who is respectful. I hate girls who talk about running away and all that stuff.

Tom, 17

Fun to be with—outgoing with a good sense of humor. I like a girl who's fun to be with.

Gene, 17

Guys appreciate girls who care about them and let them know it by being willing to listen to their problems without getting bossy or motherly. They admire girls who show respect for their families. Guys are very traditional in this respect. Maybe a guy you're going out with pictures himself married to you—and he pictures his children learning to talk to you the same way you talk to your parents. Obviously, he'll want you to be able to set a good example.

Guys love girls who can make them laugh. A good sense of humor puts a guy at ease. It indicates intelligence and intelligence is always a turn-on to a guy as long as you don't use it to try to prove you're more intelligent than he is. I was always smarter than most of the guys I dated, yet they never knew it because I made them feel special. I used my intelligence to help them to see the good things in themselves—and they loved me for it.

– FASHION TURN-ONS –

Guys are more aware of proper appearance than you might have imagined. They say:

If we go out to dinner, she should wear a skirt, not sweatpants. If a girl knows when to dress up and when to dress down, that's my kind of girl.

Donald, 18

She should dress in a unique manner—not with dirty sneakers and ripped jeans just because everyone else in her crowd dresses that way. A girl should be artistic about her clothing. When she dresses, she's painting a picture of herself—of her personality.

Joel, 16

I like a girl with sex appeal. That's not shown by wearing low-class clothing. She should dress in good taste. I mean, she should dress in a way that would not embarrass me if my parents happened to see me walking with her on the street.

Matt, 17

Guys appreciate a girl who knows the right thing to wear for the occasion. They admire a girl who is willing to be unique in her style, and they love good taste. It makes them proud to be with you rather than embarrassed and apologetic. They believe that the way a girl dresses is a reflection on them. After all, they are with her. They imagine onlookers saying: "Hey, look at that guy. He's with that fine-looking girl. He must have what it takes."

Obviously, guys are looking for more than physical beauty in a girl. They want girls who are warm and loving and who show respect for others—who have an inner beauty. I was surprised to read their answers, but only because I didn't expect teenage boys to be so mature in their awareness of what it is that really makes a girl attractive.

– I WANT A GIRL JUST LIKE THE GIRL WHO MARRIED DEAR OLD DAD –

If you really want to know how to get a guy to fall in love with you, just find out what he likes about his mother. You may have heard of the old, old song: "I want a girl, just like the girl who married dear old Dad." Psychologists agree that this is true not only for guys and their mothers but for girls and their fathers. (See page 168 of the other half of this book, "What Boys Want to Know About Girls" for a discussion on this subject). I asked guys, "Which of your mother's traits do you admire and respect and look for in a girlfriend?" They all had answers to this question.

> Her kindness. She's loving and appreciative. She's polite and smart.
>
> *Mack, 18*

> She's a lighthearted, soft-spoken lady. I love that about her.
>
> *Jesse, 17*

> I look for a responsible, truthful, caring girl, because that's what my mother is.
>
> *James, 16*

> My mother is very witty and she loves people— very sociable. I notice that the girls I really fall for have the same qualities.
>
> *Joe, 15*

> I admire my mother's determination and her daring. Any girl I'd really like could never be a stick-in-the-mud.
>
> *Dean, 14*

My mother is the cleanest, sweetest-smelling person you ever met. I like a girl to be clean and smelling good all the time.

Mickey, 17

My mother is generous, she's independent and self-confident. I could never love a girl who was calculating, clinging, or insecure.

Al, 19

I'm looking for someone with my mother's courage. I like the way she deals with problems.

Barry, 17

If your boyfriend's mother is honest, how do you think he'll feel about you if he's always catching you in lies? If she is independent and self-reliant, what will happen if you cling to him and rely on him for every little thing? If his mother is friendly and sociable, what do you think he'll feel toward you if you are reclusive and refuse to speak with people when the two of you go to a party?

I'm not suggesting that you change your personality so that it matches up with your boyfriend's mother's. Anyway, chances are, it already does to some extent, because guys are usually attracted to girls who remind them, in a good way, of their mothers. But if you find your boyfriend picking on you about a certain thing, you might try asking him some indirect questions about his mother to see if you fall short of one of the traits he admires in his mother.

This chapter was full of advice on what to avoid if you don't want to turn guys off and what to do if you want to do the reverse. Not all of it will apply to every guy you meet—of course not. There are always exceptions. But generally speaking, if you become aware of the basic themes discussed in this chapter, you'll find yourself having an easier time of attracting the guys you want. Good luck. Who ever said it was going to be easy? But it's fun!

8

The Worst Thing I Ever Did to a Girl: Guys' True Confessions

"They're all the same. Guys are just no good." Did you ever feel that way? Guys have done some extremely cruel things to girls. Why do they behave this way?

Guys often act on impulse. Instead of thinking about the consequences of their actions, they do or say what's immediately convenient. Unfortunately, their thoughtless behavior often causes you great pain.

No normal guy sets out with the goal of hurting a girl, yet so many of them do just that. As you might expect, a lot of the "worst" things have to do with sex. So read carefully to see how you can avoid being a victim.

– I REALLY USED THAT GIRL –

When a guy uses a girl just for sex, he likes to tell himself, "It's her fault, she shouldn't have let me. If she's stupid enough..." But deep down inside, he knows he's wrong and he feels guilty. Here's proof.

> The worst thing I did was get this girl to have sex with me—then never call her again. She must have felt really let down.
>
> *Willie, 17*

> After I had sex with this girl, I just got up and left without saying good-bye or kissing her good-bye. I felt awful.
>
> *Timmy, 18*

> I had sex with this girl only twice, and then she tried to say I got her pregnant. I laughed in her face. She started crying.
>
> *Jim, 16*

Whether or not these guys admit to feeling guilty, they know they did wrong, because these answers were in response to the question: "What is the worst thing you ever did to a girl?" But that's not much comfort to the girl.

A guy who never calls a girl once he has sex with her probably knew all along that he wouldn't call even though I'm sure he swore to her that he was interested in a relationship. Guys who do this know it's not right, but they're unable to resist the urge to take advantage of a weak-willed person. Be careful. There are a lot of guys like that out there. They don't plan to break your heart, (your heart isn't what's on their minds), but they do it anyway.

A guy who gets up and leaves quickly, right after having sex, obviously wants to separate himself from his actions. He wants to avoid any emotional involvement. He may even dislike the girl—and himself—for what they've just done with each other. So having achieved his goal (satisfied his sexual urge) he now wants to leave and forget it ever happened. You certainly don't want to be in a position like this—and there's only one way of making sure that you're not.

A guy who laughs in a girl's face when she tells him she's pregnant does so out of nervousness. He's really saying: "Don't try to pin it on me. I was only with you twice." Doesn't the fellow know it only takes one meeting of an egg and a sperm to cause a pregnancy? Of course he does. But his fear of the consequences causes him to imply that the girl may have had sex with lots of others. He knows that if he is the father of the child, and the girl can prove it, he's just as responsible morally, legally, and financially for the fate of that child as the mother is. See a lawyer for legal advice if you find yourself unmarried and pregnant. You're going to need all the help you can get, and a lawyer is a good place to start.

If you've been hurt by guys who have been insensitive to you, who have taken advantage of you sexually, what can you do? There's an appropriate saying in the world of gambling: "Cut your losses and move on." Okay. You were a fool. Say to yourself, "I won't make *that* mistake again," and then don't.

– I STOOD HER UP –

Sex isn't the only area in which guys can let you down. For a variety of reasons, many of them having nothing to do with your personality and everything to do with boys' insecurity and lack of maturity, boys often fail to live up to their word.

> I promised this girl I would take her to her prom, but then I decided not to go. Instead of telling her,

I kept putting it off until it was the day of the prom. I called her the same day and pretended I was sick.

Tony, 18

I made a date with this girl I had met at a club, but when the time came for the date I didn't have money, so I just stood her up. She wasn't that hot-looking, anyway.

Rob, 18

I had spent the day with this girl, and we decided to go out that night, but we wanted to change our clothes. I was supposed to go home and get dressed, and come back later that night. But when I got home, my friend called me up and told me all the guys were going to hang out. I didn't feel like going all the way back to that girl's house so I just stood her up. I didn't want to call her because I knew I would feel guilty and ruin my night if I had to lie like that on the phone. Instead I called her three days later and didn't mention it at all. Then when she brought it up, I made up an excuse about having to go somewhere with my mother.

Wayne, 17

Tony is eighteen, yet he hasn't learned to face uncomfortable situations. Instead he procrastinates, hoping that the problem will go away. He'll learn, I hope, that by avoiding problems you only make them bigger. Had he called the girl as soon as he decided not to go, it wouldn't have been a big deal. The girl would have had time to get another date, and he would have no sad tale to tell now. But like a lot of guys his age, he's not very responsible about sticking to his word.

Rob's real reason for not going on the date is lack of money. He rationalizes (makes up an inappropriate excuse) by saying: "She wasn't that hot-looking, anyway."

The fact is, Rob was too embarrassed to call the girl because he didn't want to tell her about his lack of money. He doesn't realize that he could say: "Something came up. I'm really sorry..." So instead of doing the right thing and facing the issue, he says to himself: "Forget about it, I'll just run away."

Wayne is obviously looking out for "number one" and only number one. His goal is to have the best of all possible times, and he doesn't care who he has to hurt to do it. Notice that he says he didn't call her that night to let her know that his plans had changed because "I knew I would feel guilty and ruin my night if I had to lie like that on the phone." I...I...I. He doesn't concern himself with her feelings at all. He doesn't stop to think of how let down the girl must feel, after having gotten dressed and having waited for him to show up. In short, Wayne is extremely self-centered. He's not planning to hurt anyone's feelings, but it's a safe bet that he does it quite often.

If anyone ever stands you up or breaks a promise to you, confront him and tell him straight out: "What you did was inconsiderate and immature. I'm disappointed and furious." Or something like that. You'll feel a lot better because at least you will have expressed your anger and frustration. You may even have saved yourself medical problems later in life. (Doctors are now in agreement that many diseases have their origin in stress and unexpressed anger. So let it out on the one who caused it. Why should you suffer alone?)

– YOU ALWAYS HURT THE ONE YOU LOVE –

Guys can be rude or thoughtless to girls they don't know very well, and they can take advantage of them sexually. But often the worst things they do are to their girlfriends because their feelings about them can get so intense. I know that it's not much of a comfort to know that he hurt you so much because he loved you so much, but you should be aware of how powerful these emotions can be. Sometimes, you may want to change your behavior if you think you started the trouble. Other times, you may decide that no matter who set the trouble in motion, your boyfriend's reaction to it is excessive and unacceptable. Violent behavior should certainly make you think twice.

Leigh, 17, is a jealous guy. He says:

> The other day my girlfriend was hugging and kissing some guy. He was a friend, I later found out, but at the time, it looked much more intimate than that. Also, it was out in the street. I grabbed her by the neck and dragged her down the street exclaiming, "What the ——— is your problem, you freak!"

Leigh was embarrassed when he found out that the guy was just a good friend. He felt like a fool. His girl could be flattered that he cares so much, but if I were she, I would feel threatened by a guy who acts before he finds out the full story. If your boyfriend is quick-tempered, give him one more chance, but if it happens a second time, leave him. You don't want anyone to be "struck out" the third time.

Bobby, 18, admits:

> The worst thing I ever did to my girl was push her. She got me real mad, so I just sort of shoved her and left. I didn't really want to, but my mind was telling me to slap her. I don't like raising my hand to a girl, so I pushed her instead.

Bobby realizes his potential for violence. I hope his girlfriend does, too. A guy like Bobby is likely to get more violent the next time. If I were Bobby's girl, I'd tell him two things: 1. Good-bye. 2. Get help.

Here's how Jeff, 17, dealt with his girlfriend when they had a fight.

> I got so mad at my girlfriend that I left her at the Oak Beach Inn, with no way of getting home.

Jeff gave in to a moment of rage. His action was extremely inconsiderate. If I were his girlfriend, I'd give him one more chance. But if he does anything like that again, it means he thinks he has a right to punish you when things don't go his way. Who needs a guy like that? Drop him.

– I REALLY PAID HER BACK –

Since guys often hide their true feelings for you in an attempt to appear "cool" and "macho," it's sometimes a shock when they show great emotion and do something vindictive toward the end of the relationship. You might have thought they didn't even care. What a shame to have to find out this way.

> I cheated on this girl eighteen times in one month because I found out she had been with someone else. Then I told her and broke up with her.
> *Charlie, 18*

> I went out with this girl and when she broke up with me, I invited her to my house, pretending that I wanted to talk about getting back together. In the meantime, I had another girl over. When she arrived, I had my brother answer the door. He told her I was in my room. When she got there I was kissing the girl.
> *Ray, 17*

My girlfriend told me she wanted to see other guys, and when she came over to my house to return some of my gold jewelry and other things, I grabbed them from her, slammed the door in her face, and told her to stay out of my life.

Don, 16

Charlie, Ray, and Don are hurting, so they seek a way to get revenge on the girl who caused the pain. If one of your boyfriends does something cruel toward the end of the relationship, it probably means he's been holding back a lot of emotions. He's angry, and now that the relationship is ending he wants to "pay you back." Instead of allowing his misguided efforts to get to you, ask him why he's so angry. He may tell you how he really feels, and the two of you can at least part company without hating each other. It's always a shame to let a relationship with someone you care about end in such a way that you can't even respect each other.

If you're too angry to confront him about his cruel actions, then realize that any guy who goes to such great extremes to hurt you is hurting pretty badly himself. He's in a lot of pain—and that pain involves unresolved feelings about you. Try to forgive him. But even more important, try to forget him.

When your mother told you, "There's more than one fish in the sea," she was so right. Don't waste your time trying to make up with someone who's treated you badly. If you can't break up on good terms, then just leave him to his hatred. He may have problems that only a professional can help with.

9

What Moms and Dads Tell Their Sons About Girls

Whether or not we realize it, our view of the opposite sex is greatly influenced by our parents. Mothers and fathers all have their favorite lectures on what to look for and what to "watch out for" when it comes to dating.

In this chapter, you'll get the inside story on what fathers and mothers say to their sons about girls. Perhaps after reading these remarks, you'll understand a little more about why guys have certain attitudes about women.

– LECTURES FATHERS GIVE SONS –

Fathers like to believe that their sons are a "chip off the old block." Maybe this is why they're so concerned about the way their sons behave with the opposite sex. They see it as an indirect reflection of the way they treat women.

Never Hit a Woman

Darryl's father says:

> Behave like a gentleman. Never hit a woman. A woman is for loving, not beating.
>
> *Darryl, 17*

Darryl's father tells him what any normal guy should already know. Yet his father lectures him, just to make sure he never raises his hand to a woman. Can you imagine what happens when a father says things like: "You've got to keep them in line. Every now and then you've got to give them a good slap." Sooner or later, that guy is going to hit a woman. The way to make sure it's not you is to find out more about the guy's family life. Chances are, if there's wife beating in that family, there will be wife beating in his.

If You Get a Girl Pregnant You'll Have to Sell Your Car and Start Buying Pampers.

Fathers want to make sure their sons don't ruin their lives by an accidental pregnancy or an early marriage. They say things like:

> When you grow up you're gonna want to drive a car and have fun. If you get a girl pregnant, you'll have to sell your car and start buying Pampers.
>
> *Manuel, 17*

> Make sure you use an umbrella so it doesn't rain on your parade.
>
> *Tom, 17*

> You're too young to get serious. Don't get involved with just one girl. Go out and have a good time.
>
> *Kenny, 17*

Manuel's father got married when he and Manuel's mother found out they were going to have a baby—Manuel. From that day on it was nothing but struggle and hard times for them. They're not sorry that Manuel was born, but they wish they had planned their children so that their lives wouldn't have been as hard. Manuel's father probably remembers all the things he had to give up once he found out his girl was pregnant, and he wants a better life for his son.

Tom's father uses humor to warn Tom to use protection so that there won't be an accidental pregnancy. He's smart to tell his son to be responsible for birth control. Since guys are legally responsible for a pregnancy caused by them, they shouldn't leave it all up to the girl.

Kenny's father warns him about seeing too much of one girl because he knows that strong emotions can develop and lead to an early marriage. Unlike teenagers, his father has enough experience to know that once the romantic wedding day is over and the honeymoon is passed, marriage is no dream world. It's a lot of responsibility and it means you're tied down to one person—whether you feel like being tied down or not. He knows that teenagers don't realize this yet (how could they, they've never experienced marriage) and that they'll be much happier if they keep their freedom during their teen years. Kenny will probably live at least fifty years beyond his teens (according to projected life-expectancy estimates), so he'll have plenty of time in which to shoulder the responsibilities of marriage. By comparison the teen years are very brief; Kenny's father would like to see him enjoy them.

Watch Out for the Vamps

Fathers are concerned that their sons watch out for sex-related diseases:

> Don't kiss a girl with cold sores.
>
> *John, 15*

Wear a condom. If you don't, you can catch AIDS. Take a shower right after you have sex.

Jose, 15

The zipper is the problem. Not the condom. Just keep your zipper up, and you don't have to worry about anything.

Errol, 16

Watch out for the vamps. They can spread disease.

Troy, 18

Herpes, gonorrhea, syphilis, and now the worst disease of all—AIDS. It really is a jungle out there—and fathers know that their sons can lose their lives or damage their reproductive potential by making just one foolish move.

– LECTURES MOTHERS GIVE SONS –

Mothers' lectures are different from fathers' lectures. A mother wants her son to take out nice girls and to treat them well. She wants him to get married and have children—but not too soon. And she doesn't want any girl to take advantage of her son, so she warns him about girls who might push him around or be after his money.

Marry a Virgin

Chances are, your mother was a virgin when she got married. So your boyfriend's mother probably was, too. Mothers know that today many girls have lost their virginity by their early teens, but most mothers just don't respect such girls. If they were virgins when they got married, they want their sons to marry a girl with standards as high as their own. And if they weren't virgins, they may regret not having been able to give their husbands the gift of their virginity and may wish better for their sons. They don't want their sons to marry a girl who's been "around the block" too many times. They want the very best for their sons and encourage them to:

Find a nice respectable girl who is a virgin.
Billy, 17

Guys won't admit this to their girlfriends (especially if they're trying to convince them that it's okay to have sex), but they take their mothers' advice to heart. They think it would be a dream come true if they could marry one. (See pp. 48–49 for direct quotes from guys on this subject.)

You Wouldn't Want a Guy to Abuse Your Sister

Mothers are even more sensitive than fathers when it comes to counseling their sons on the right way to treat a woman. Maybe they remember how it feels to be treated disrespectfully by a guy. According to their sons, mothers say:

Be nice to girls and don't use them.
Mike, 18

Treat a girl the way your father treats me.
Richie, 19

Remember, you wouldn't want a guy to abuse your sister—so treat girls with respect.
Dom, 16

If you don't like a girl, then don't lead her on, because it hurts.

Tom, 18

Thank God some mothers do give these lectures. It's advice like this that helps to give guys a conscience. Mike, Richie, Dom, and Tom may treat girls badly from time to time, but you can be sure of one thing: They'll feel plenty guilty about it as their mothers' words ring in their ears. Chances are, in the long run, after making a few mistakes, they'll treat women with a lot of respect. But guys who don't get this message from either of their parents may be bad news. That's one reason it's sometimes a good idea to get to know a guy's parents.

Be a Gentleman About It: Don't Tell Everybody

Mothers talk to their sons about sex, but their concern goes beyond pregnancy and health issues. Because they know the kind of sexual pressures a lot of boys put on girls, they want their sons to be sensitive to girls' feelings, and they hope their sons will have enough self-control to wait awhile before their first sexual experience. They say:

If you have sex with a girl, be a gentleman about it and don't go tell everybody.

Dave, 17

Don't rush into sex. There's nothing wrong with waiting until you're older.

Paulie, 17

Dave's mother can't stand guys who "kiss and tell." Maybe this happened to her or one of her friends when she was a teenager. In any case, her advice is excellent.

Girls don't respect guys who are insensitive enough to go around bragging about sexual conquests.

Why Guys Think They're Not a Man if They Are Virgins

More mothers and fathers should lecture their sons to wait—not just until they're older but until they're married. I only found one teenager whose parent gave such a lecture. No wonder so many boys think they're "not a man" if they haven't had sex by the time they're sixteen (and most of them younger).

I don't have a son, but if I did, I would tell him to wait until he's married. I'll bet you laughed when you read that. See what I mean—see how deeply ingrained the double standard is. Even girls subscribe to it, and you're the ones who are hurt by it. When you think about it, it's ridiculous. If girls don't have sex until they're married, but boys think they're supposed to have sex whenever they can get it, then who is going to have sex with all these young studs? It's a total contradiction, isn't it. Ridiculous.

Don't Let the Girls Boss You Around

Why would a mother say something like:

> Watch out for aggressive girls.
> *Jared, 17*

To a mother, an "aggressive" girl means a girl who is going to control her son and take him away from her. It's every woman's nightmare that her son will marry such a girl, because once a domineering wife takes control of her son, she will probably want to use her power to make him forget his mother. Bossy girls don't like competition, which means he won't be able to visit his mother after he gets married, he won't ask for her advice, he won't even call anymore. In fact, he may have to forget she exists. If her son marries a "nice, loving" girl, however, the mother feels safe. That kind of girl won't compete with a mother, but will encourage her husband to visit his mother, to be a good son, to keep in touch, and so forth.

Mothers are right to be concerned about who their sons go out with, fall in love with, and marry. Isn't it true that you will have an influence on your future husband?

Make Sure She Wants You, Not Your Wallet

> Don't let a girl take you for your money. Be careful.
>
> *Mark, 17*

Mothers remember how easy it was to use a guy for his money. Some of them did it themselves. If a mother imagines her precious son is being taken advantage of in this way, it drives her crazy. No mother wants to see her son made a "sucker." If you've ever gone out with a guy you didn't really like just because he had lots of money and was eager to spend it on you, you're the one his mother is warning him about. Many girls have done this at one time or another, but soon realize that they are hurting themselves as much as they are hurting the boy they are "using"—that they are lowering their self-esteem (what they think of themselves). You should go out with guys you are attracted to because of their personality, values, and physical attributes. Money should not be your only concern.

Do the lectures guys get from their parents affect their minds? Do they influence the way guys react to the opposite sex? Definitely so. No matter how much guys put their parents down and rebel against them, they are deeply affected by their parents' values. Your boyfriend belonged to his parents first. And chances are his relationship with them will outlast his relationship with you. It should come as no surprise to you to learn how important their opinion is to him, whether he's willing to admit it or not.

We all constantly measure others against the values we have been taught by our parents. In our earlier years, these are the *only* values we respect. Eventually, we may learn to weigh our parents' advice against other ideas we're exposed to—through friends, books we've read, movies we've seen, television shows we've viewed, or experiences we've had. With the help of these other influences, we finally formulate a philosophy that is our own, but we never completely escape the influence of our parents.

You can see, then, how your boyfriend's view of women is bound to be affected by the values of his parents. Wouldn't it be fun to find out what they say to him? You can probably figure most of it out just by thinking about how your boyfriend treats girls. Think of some of the comments he's made and the way he reacts to you in certain situations. Then imagine the lectures that may be behind such conduct. I'll bet you came up with at least one that is correct. Just for fun, ask him what his mother and father are always warning him about when it comes to girls. See if you're right.

10

How to Get and Keep the Guy of Your Dreams

The best way to get and keep the guy of your dreams is to become the kind of girl every guy dreams of. What kind of a girl is that? One who follows the "Ten Commandments of Love." I composed them by summarizing everything the guys I talked to said they loved in the girls they know. Here they are:

1. Thou shalt be friendly and not stuck-up.
2. Thou shalt not talk like a truck driver.
3. Thou shalt be understanding and kind.
4. Thou shalt not dress like a dirtbag or a slut.
5. Thou shalt compliment him regularly.
6. Thou shalt not nag him about spending time with his friends.
7. Thou shalt forgive him.
8. Thou shalt not play him for a fool.
9. Thou shalt stop being so suspicious.
10. Thou shalt not compare him unfavorably to other guys.

The next time you meet a guy you like and seem to be having trouble getting him to ask you out, or the next time you find yourself fighting a lot with your boyfriend, review the above list and see if you're breaking any of the commandments. If you're honest with yourself, you may find the answer.

Of course there's no guarantee that by following the above guidelines you'll get or keep *every* guy you want. Let's face it, you're not every guy's "type," no matter how beautiful or terrific you are, and not everyone is compatible. But the ten commandments will greatly increase your odds.

You may be saying, "Hey, what about the guys? They should learn some commandments of love, too." Don't worry. They are given some definite instructions by you ladies. If you're curious to see what girls have to say about guys, turn to the second half of this book, "What Boys Want to Know About Girls." Then make sure your boyfriend reads it, too. It can't hurt your relationship—and it may help.

And don't forget to write to me if you have any questions.

Part 2
What Boys Want to Know About Girls

1

Jealousy and Cheating: Why?

Girls are *really* jealous. All you have to do is look at another girl and they assume you're thinking about cheating. If you're late, they immediately begin to wonder if you're with another girl, and if they see telephone numbers in your wallet, you're lost. This is what boys have told me about girls. Doesn't it sound familiar?

Why are girls so suspicious, so jealous? Could it be that they themselves are guilty of what they suspect you of—cheating? Don't read any further if you can't take pain. What you will read in the second half of this chapter, when we get to the subject of cheating, may be more than you can handle. But first let's talk about jealousy.

– I START THINKING MAYBE SHE HAS SOMETHING I DON'T HAVE –

When you ask them, girls seem to have plenty of reasons for being jealous, but often those reasons have more to do with their feelings about themselves than with anything you're doing.

> Most of the time I figure he's probably talking about getting something going between them, and I want to walk over and stop it before it starts, but I'm afraid of making an ass of myself.
>
> *Monique, 15*

> I don't know what he's talking about, and I'm always afraid he may have had something with her in the past. This makes me want to grill him about her later, and I usually do it, too, and we end up in a fight over it.
>
> *Floria, 17*

> I'm insecure, so right away I think he's found someone better. Then I start thinking, why am I so fat, why am I so ugly. . . .
>
> *Marlene, 16*

> I'm just jealous. I start thinking maybe *she* has something I don't have.
>
> *Emily, 18*

If you read between the lines, you can see that it isn't really *you* they doubt—it's themselves. They're insecure about their ability to hold on to you as a boyfriend. Instead of getting angry, why not be flattered that they think you so attractive that other girls would want to steal you. And then, to make them feel more sure of themselves and less jealous, say something like: "You're one in a million. No one could possibly take your place in my life."

– WHY DO GIRLS ALWAYS ASSUME YOU'VE BEEN WITH ANOTHER GIRL IF YOU'RE LATE? –

Perhaps it's the same kind of insecurity we just talked about, plus a little anger, that causes them to give you the third degree when you're late. Here's what girls say about why they ask a million questions before they let a guy off the hook for making them wait.

> Simply because I don't trust him!
> *Rosemary, 16*

> Because he starts to get tongue-tied and looks nervous. He gives himself away.
> *Dorothy, 17*

> I suspect he was with another girl because he wants to be a playboy and I know it.
> *Deena, 17*

> I want to give him a hard time to teach him a lesson about showing up when he's supposed to.
> *Lee, 15*

> The jackass made me wait when I could be with a responsible guy who keeps his plans, and I want him to know how mad I am.
> *Marthe, 15*

– SHE FOUND TELEPHONE NUMBERS IN YOUR WALLET –

To show you how jealous most girls are, and what they're capable of doing if they think you might be cheating on them, I posed the question: "If you found telephone numbers in your boyfriend's wallet, what would you do and why?"

> I would copy the numbers on a paper and call every one of them to find out who each one is.
>
> *Nancy, 17*

> Rip them up, plain and simple. He shouldn't have any girls' numbers in his wallet.
>
> *Lois, 16*

> I would ask him about the numbers and if he didn't know what to say, I would tell him to go to hell and kick him out of my house.
>
> *Lorena, 17*

> Bring out my black book and start making some calls of my own.
>
> *Ro, 17*

> I would feel hurt, but I couldn't really do anything since the guy and I aren't married.
>
> *Cyndi, 18*

> I wouldn't freak out unless it was a perfumed piece of paper with lipstick on it and "call me any time" in quotes.
>
> *Lisa, 17*

As you can see, some girls would immediately assume the worst (the really jealous ones) and not even give you a chance to explain. Others would let you explain, but they would listen to your answer very carefully and study your body language for signs of guilt. Others would do nothing, but would silently hold it against you.

– DO GIRLS THINK THEIR BOYFRIENDS CHEAT ON THEM? –

We already know that girls are always afraid that guys are planning to cheat on them, but do they really, truly believe that will happen?

> No way. He's too much in love with me.
> *Marthe, 15*

> No. No. No. We spend all our time together. When would he get the chance?
> *Stacey, 17*

> I know he doesn't. He really isn't the kind of guy who cheats. I have him figured.
> *Jana, 16*

> He wouldn't dare. He knows better than to make that dumb mistake. If he did I would hunt him down like a hound dog.
> *Susan, 17*

> I doubt it. I'm not with him every minute so I can't swear to it—and he is very cute, but I really doubt it.
> *Tanya, 17*

Why do the girls state so adamantly that they believe you don't cheat on them? Possibly it is a form of wishful thinking. On top of that, there's the very human tendency to want to have one's cake—and eat it, too. You may recognize this pattern of thinking in yourself. Do you cheat on your girlfriend, guard her jealously, yet believe that she doesn't cheat on you?

But if girls don't think you cheat, why are they so suspicious and jealous? It could be because they cheat, or at least want to—so they assume you are thinking about cheating, too. In psychological terms, this thought process is called "projection." A person who projects will assign to you the motive she herself is guilty of.

– DO GIRLS SEE OTHERS ON THE SIDE WHEN THEY'RE GOING STEADY? –

Obviously, the answer to this question varies from girl to girl, but if girls are so alert to the possibility of your cheating on them, even though they don't really think you do, you can't help wondering if it's because they cheat on you. You would think that they would be sensitive to your feelings since they're so easily hurt by the thought of your infidelities. Other guys should be the last thing on their minds. Well, it doesn't work that way.

When I asked girls if they see anyone on the side while they are going out with a guy, here's what they said:

> Yes, because I get tired of seeing the same face every day.
>
> *Nicky, 16*

> Why not? I'm probably not the only one he's seeing.
>
> *Lavette, 17*

> My friends all do it, so why shouldn't I?
>
> *China, 16*

I only see my boyfriend on Saturday and Sunday, so I need to fill in Monday through Friday.

Yvette, 17

I always do—at the end of a relationship. ——— him. He treated me like dirt for however long, now I'm going to get him where it hurts.

Joan, 15

That's right. You read correctly. They do it because they get bored with *you* just the way you get bored with them (see p. 6 in the other half of this book, "What Girls Want to Know About Boys,") and also to get even with you for cheating on or mistreating them.

– HOW MUCH GUILT DO GIRLS FEEL WHEN THEY CHEAT ON YOU? –

When I asked girls if they feel guilty about cheating, the answers seemed to be: "Not at all." I asked them if they thought it was right and normal to see other guys and not tell you about it. Here's what they said.

When you're a teenager, you don't want to be limited to just one guy. It's fun to meet other people and it's normal. You may really like your boyfriend and want to keep him, but you don't want to feel boxed in, so you hang out with other guys once in a while.

Simone, 15

You are young. Live it up, for God's sake. Marriage is a while down the road.

Dominica, 16

It doesn't make sense to really be true to a guy too early in life. We are young and we want to enjoy the company of other guys.

Allie, 17

One guy is not enough to be everything to me.

Sandra, 16

– WHY GIRLS DON'T TELL THE TRUTH ABOUT THE "OTHER GUYS" –

Well, you might ask, "If the girls think it's right to see others, why can't they be honest and tell me about it instead of going behind my back?" According to the girls, the answer is very clear.

Guys are very possessive. They could *never* handle it. You may really need some space. You miss the guys you were good friends with and used to hang out with. When I met my boyfriend, that was the end of all my male friends. I miss the fun, so...

Marthe, 15

They take it that you don't care about them anymore or they think they aren't good-looking enough to hold you, so I don't want to hurt their feelings.

Jennifer, 15

You don't want him to think you're a slut or that you just went out with him for his money, so you have to lie and see them behind his back.

Ramona, 17

If I told him the truth, then *he* would do it, too, and maybe he would leave me for another girl.
Mary, 16

He might rearrange my face.
Monique, 17

– IS IT OKAY TO CHEAT? –

Can you understand the problem? Girls feel boxed in and tied down when they limit themselves to seeing only one guy, yet they can't be honest with their boyfriends about their need to see others because they feel the guy wouldn't understand. He'd feel rejected, call them names, call it quits, or even get violent. So girls "cheat." But is it really cheating, or is it actually normal teenage behavior? I find it interesting that just as the girls think it's normal teenage behavior, so do the boys, but only for them—not for their girlfriends. (See p. 10–11 of the other half of this book, "What Girls Want to Know About Boys.")

What is the answer to the dilemma of "cheating"? For starters, I don't think we should use the word *cheating* at all. *Exploring* would be a better word.

Teenagers are learning a lot about love and relationships all at once, and this usually creates a problem. On the one hand, you are beginning to learn how to form a deep and lasting bond with someone of the opposite sex; the boyfriend-girlfriend situation is a sort of rehearsal for adult love. But on the other hand, it is only a rehearsal, it's seldom the real thing, and part of this experiment should consist of exploring and sorting through other relationships until you find someone who is right for you. The time to do all this exploring and measuring is in the teen years—not after you're married.

If you are seeing someone other than your girlfriend and she doesn't know about it, or if she is doing the same to you, you are simply playing the game normal adolescents play—the game of growing up and learning what is and isn't right for you in a relationship. My feeling is that, in the interest of honesty and trust, it would be better to change the rules of the game and figure out a modified version of going steady in which you spend most of your dating time with each other but are free to see others on occasion, too. You need not make an official announcement to each other when you do see someone else. It would be an unspoken understanding, because "telling" each other each time would perhaps be too provocative and might cause an argument. Such an arrangement would be good for both of you, because it would help you to avoid getting into the habit of infidelity by providing an honorable arrangement that is agreeable and fair to both of you.

2

Love, Romance, and Relationships: How Girls Feel

By now you've probably discovered that most girls want a lot more love and romance than you are willing to give. In general women are more romantic than men (there are, of course, exceptions, and we women thank God for every one we meet). Most girls can't get enough of moonlight and roses and live for the times when you say "I love you."

– WHY GIRLS NEED TO HEAR THE WORDS "I LOVE YOU" –

Boys think it's weird that girls always ask their boyfriends to say "I love you," because they figure it should be obvious from the way they behave. But girls are never satisfied with that. They want to actually *hear* the spoken words. Here's why.

> I just like the way "I love you" sounds, especially when I'm in a bad mood. If a boy says it then, it

can get me out of the dumps—and make me feel special when nothing else can.

Kim, 15

It makes me feel he's thinking about us.

Joan, 16

I need to hear him say it so I know he's not just using me for my body.

Monique, 18

If he shows it but doesn't say it, it makes you wonder if you're reading his signals right. Maybe he just acts that way with everyone.

Lisa, 17

I get insecure. I need to hear him say it. Then I know I'm not imagining that he loves me—I have proof.

Joelle, 16

Maybe girls need to hear those words because they are more emotionally committed to the relationship than boys are. Since girls mature emotionally about two years faster than boys do, they are ready for an in-depth relationship earlier than most boys.

But even if you're seeing a girl two years younger than you, she is likely to expect more from you emotionally than you are ready to give. Why? Women, in general, give more of themselves in a love relationship than a man does. Our society has traditionally expected men to control their emotions in order to appear "manly" or strong. Unfortunately, this has caused many men to become unable to express *any* emotion for fear of seeming effeminate, which is too bad for them—it's terrible not to be able to express emotions even when you really want to—and awful for whomever they're involved with.

Not hearing any kind of affection expressed can cause a girl to feel very insecure about a relationship. Some couples even break up because of such a lack of communication, despite the fact that they really love each other. When that happens, it's really a tragedy. But that's an extreme example. Usually guys are just much more reserved than girls want them to be, and both sides have to learn to compromise in their expectations of each other.

In a sense, you're right to be careful about making declarations about love to a girl. Since girls are very sensitive when it comes to love and romance, words of love are taken very seriously by them—and they'll expect you to mean what you say and to back it up with your actions. But that doesn't mean you shouldn't sometimes be affectionate and appreciative. There are ways of making a girl feel cared for without saying "I love you."

– WHY DOES YOUR GIRLFRIEND MAKE UP THINGS TO GET YOU JEALOUS? –

In any boy-girl relationship, certain games are played. Often girls will pretend they were out for a night on the town when they were actually spending the evening at a girlfriend's or at home watching TV. Here's why.

> If he has this exciting life while I'm at home, I'm afraid maybe he'll say to himself, "She would be nowhere without me."
>
> *Jennifer, 15*

I try to get him jealous to see what he says and find out if he really cares.

Tiffany, 16

Maybe he's bragging about what *he* did and I want to look good, too—so I soup myself up by telling him all these great things I did without him.

Margie, 16

Say he went out one weekend without me and had a wild time—I don't want him thinking I sat home waiting for him.

Amber, 15

To make myself look better.

Serena, 13

Don't you do the same thing once in a while? It's human nature to try to protect your ego. You don't want to look as if you have nothing going on in your life, so you invent a whole story. It's not a good idea to get into the habit of making things up—but most of us have done it a few times. Later we realized that it wasn't necessary. We learn that there's no shame in admitting that our life is not always partying and good times, and that sometimes we just sit at home watching TV or reading a good book. Let's face it, no one in this world, not even celebrities, is doing something exciting every minute. But some girls haven't learned that yet, so try to understand.

– WHY DO GIRLS BRAG ABOUT OTHER GUYS THEY'VE DATED? –

Did a girl you were seeing ever start bragging about all the other "fine" guys she's gone out with? Why do girls do this? Don't they know it's the last thing you want to hear? They may know, but they don't care. They're more concerned with giving you a message, and here it is:

> I want him to know that he'd better treat me right. I've got to teach him that there are ten hot guys just waiting for me to break up with him.
> *Marthe, 15*

> It makes me feel good about myself. In my mind I say, "Hey, you got it."
> *Mona, 18*

> To remind him that if he gets stupid, there are plenty of others ready to grab me.
> *Randy, 17*

> When he's not acting right, I remember how well other guys treated me and I miss them. I want to talk about it to let him know I don't have to take his ———.
> *Sally, 16*

> I think I can get any guy, and I like to let him know it.
> *Lucy, 14*

It seems clear that girls want to remind you that other guys appreciate them, too—just in case you don't. If your girl is doing this, I'd be willing to bet that it's because you aren't acting as if you are honored and delighted to be going out with her. Maybe you've started to take her for granted, or maybe you started bragging about other girls you've been with. The next time a girl you date starts talking about others, see if you are guilty of the same or haven't done enough to let her know you think she's special.

– BREAKING UP—DO THEY LIE ABOUT THE REASON? –

No matter how old you are, I'm sure you've already had this experience: Your girlfriend told you she wants to break up, but the reason she gave sounded phony. Boys want to know: "Do girls tell us the real reason why they want to break up, or do they make up excuses?"

I tell the truth. Lies are more painful in the end.
Diane, 17

I get right to the point. The jackass should know what he did wrong. He deserves to hear his faults and then some.
Rose, 15

I like to be honest. This way he can realize that the has to change his ways with girls—improve himself in the future.
Johanna, 16

I can't be blunt. I beat around the bush. Then if that doesn't work, I tell him why.
Lisa, 17

I just stop calling him.
Nicky, 16

I use the excuse "my parents don't want me to get serious."
Candy, 18

I told a guy I was going away with my grandparents to Puerto Rico for a while and I didn't know when I was coming back. I didn't want to hurt his feeings.
Carmen, 14

You can probably tell when a girl is lying about why she wants to break up. If I were being lied to, I would become angry and demand to know the real reason. For me, the truth is necessary in order to let go of a relationship.

Everyone is different, however. Some people don't really want to know why. They believe it would be too painful. If you think the girl is making up excuses, decide whether or not you feel it's necessary for you to ferret out the full story. If it is, you can say something like: "I know you don't want to hurt my feelings, but I would appreciate it if you could tell me the real reason...." If, however, you feel you don't need to know, let the girl off the hook by allowing her to think you believed her story. Also, keep in mind that often there is no real reason. At all ages, it's possible to fall into and out of love for reasons no one can explain—so why should your girlfriend be able to? This kind of changeableness is particularly common in the teenage years.

– ROMANCE: HOW TO PLEASE A GIRL –

We've been talking about love, but what about romance? What is romance, anyway? It's the unexpected, the exotic, the unusual—the impractical. The girls can give specifics about what it means to them. I asked them: "What is the most romantic thing a guy could do for you?" They are quite willing to give away their secret desires.

> He could buy me roses and take me for a long walk on the beach to watch the sun set.
>
> *Kim, 15*

I dream of a day when he will take me to a quiet restaurant with soft music and expensive champagne.

Dolores, 16

Let's take a walk in the park—along the river, then sit on the benches and talk and kiss.

Patrice, 17

I wish he would take me to a tropical paradise and walk under the stars, after a moonlit picnic under a palm tree.

Iris, 14

We could have a very spontaneous moment with Dom Perignon and candlelight.

Tricia, 19

I wish he would buy me gardenias and tell me from his heart that he loves me.

Erin, 17

Bring me flowers for no reason at all.

Jeanie, 16

When we are arguing and I am talking too much, just grab me and kiss me all over.

Rosemary, 17

Ask me to marry him.

Gloria, 15

Could you do any of the above for your girlfriend? Notice that the key to romance is the unplanned and spontaneous element. It wouldn't do to tell your girl ahead of time, "I'm going to send you flowers," or to brag about the bargain you got in shopping around for them. That would ruin it completely.

Most of the requests are not very expensive, you

know. Just one rose will make the point and possibly be even more romantic than a dozen, and how much does it cost to walk along the beach? "But I'm not romantic," you say. So what? You may find yourself becoming romantic as you try these things out. In the beginning it will seem like a game, but once you get into it, you may surprise yourself by finding yourself enjoying romance. You may be more romantic than you thought.

In any case, if you ever fall madly in love with a girl and she doesn't seem to be quite as in love with you, try some of the suggestions above that are appropriate for you, and I can practically guarantee that you will see a *big* change in her attitude.

– DO GIRLS WANT TO GET MARRIED? –

We've talked about love and romance. What's left? Marriage. All three go together—or at least they should. Most girls want to get married, but not all of them are eager to make that commitment—at least not too soon.

> I've always dreamed of marriage, but not until thirty. I want to live my life first.
>
> *Monique, 17*

> Yes. I want to have a family to love and to love me back—but not until I achieve my goals in life.
>
> *Rosa, 18*

> No way. I see what my mother went through to get divorced.
>
> *Michelle, 14*

> Never. It's too much responsibility.
>
> *Maxine, 14*

Yes, because if I fall in love with a guy, I want to spend my life with him—at the age of forty-five.
Dorene, 17

Some girls feel they want to get married; others believe they don't. But chances are, even the girls who say they don't want to get married will meet someone like you—someone so irresistible that they will change their minds. Your warmth, charm, and love may disarm them of all of their defenses. Don't forget, to a woman, asking her to marry you not only means you love her. It is also the most romantic thing in the world.

3

Arguments: I Say Black—She Says White!

What do you and your girl argue about? *Everything*. You want to go here—she wants to go there. You do something to her—she wants revenge and does the same thing to you. You do or do not do certain things. She nags you about them. Everything is going well and suddenly, for no apparent reason, she changes her mood and develops an "attitude." These situations often result in the kind of blowup that can end a relationship. But often there weren't any important issues at stake; it was just that tempers got out of control and neither person knew how to stop the fight before it turned really ugly. The key to keeping the peace is stopping an argument early, and to do that you need to be able to read between the lines of what's being said. If she's being bossy, maybe it's to protect herself from looking like your "slave." If she suddenly puts you down for no apparent reason, maybe it's because of something you did the night before. Learn to analyze what's really going on in your girlfriend's mind when she's being difficult. Sometimes you can stop a fight and save a relationship.

(Other times, of course, you may *want* it to end—especially if the girl is moody and unreasonable a lot of the time.) No one wants to spend hours trying to decipher someone else's moods every day. But it's worth doing every now and then if you really care for her and she usually treats you well.

– WHY GIRLS ARGUE WITH YOU SO MUCH –

They argue for various reasons. Here are some of them:

> Usually the argument starts when *he* says or does something stupid.
>
> *Theresa, 16*

> I like to play the devil's advocate and challenge his statements.
>
> *Lisa, 17*

> People just get like that. I think most girls do it because of P.M.S. [pre-menstrual syndrome].
>
> *Kimmie, 15*

> I argue with my present boyfriend because we are total opposites—we have very different values.
>
> *Marthe, 15*

> Just to bug his nerves. I don't want him to think whatever he says goes.
>
> *Mandy, 16*

> Because I like to be right all the time and he knows it.
>
> *Rosemary, 16*

It brings us closer together. If we never argued, I would never know what he was all about.

Randy, 17

Many of the girls say they argue because they believe they're right or because they need to have the last word. Actually, it's quite normal for teenagers (boys as well as girls) to take a strong stand about what may seem to adults to be a minor issue. They do this because they're just beginning to form their own beliefs and values, and when someone opposes an idea they have, they experience it as a threat. Why? Teenagers are not yet really sure of their own ideas, so they argue to protect them—and, in a sense, their developing "selves."

Some girls argue to get a reaction from you. As Randy says, it's the only way she gets to know how her boyfriend thinks.

– WHY DO GIRLS DEMAND THEIR OWN WAY? –

Boys complain that girls are unreasonable in demanding their own way. Why do they do this?

Doesn't everyone?

Simone, 15

Because I want to feel in control.

Cyndi, 18

I'm used to getting my way. He doesn't know I'm getting it because I pretend to compromise—but I manipulate the situation.

Lisa, 17

My way is the best way and we'll have more fun my way.

Stacey, 17

Because I'm spoiled. My parents give me everything and I expect my boyfriend to do the same. If he really loves me the way he says he does, he would!

Lois, 16

They want their way for the same reasons you probably want your way—because it's more fun to call the shots, isn't it? So you can expect girls to continue to fight for their way just as you will continue to fight for yours. This type of arguing is part of the normal power struggle that will always take place between males and females. I say compromise is the key. If you put your mind to it, you can negotiate just about anything.

– WHY DO GIRLS ARGUE ABOUT WHERE TO GO? –

One of the favorite themes for a hot argument is: "Where will we go tonight?" Why do girls demand their own way when the question of where the two of you will spend the day or the evening comes up?

If we hang out with his stupid friends who take so long to decide where we should go, I have to go home before we get going. It seems like to him, it's okay to just hang out and do nothing. I get bored waiting around. I'd rather go to the latest movie or rent a video or go someplace.

Amber, 15

Maybe I'm bored with his selection. He wants to go to the drag races every single night. My idea of a good time is more like going out to dinner with another couple.

Myra, 17

Why should he get his way? I think we should compromise and do some of the things we both want, or at least we should take turns on doing what he wants and what I want.

Deena, 16

He's too lazy to think of something adventurous, so he claims he wants to hang out at the local ice-cream place. But when I push him into it, he goes for a ride with me to the amusement park or the beach, or someplace more exciting.

Tara, 16

It looks as if girls are not satisfied with just "hanging out" with the same crowd, in the same place, every night. They'd rather be doing a variety of things (going to movies, watching videos, visiting an amusement park, eating at a restaurant, etc.). On the surface, it would seem as if their boyfriends are simply too boring for them, but that's only on *the surface*. The real story is, the boys are quite content to hang out with their friends—even when they are with their girlfriends—while the girls, whether they realize it or not, are requesting that their boyfriends separate themselves from the crowd of friends they always hang around with and spend special or at least semispecial time with them. (For example, special time would be to go off to an amusement park alone with the girl or with another couple and the girl, and semispecial time would be to involve the whole crowd in doing something different for a change.) Boys do like to spend more time with their friends than with their girlfriends, and I've explained this to the girls in the other half of this book, "What Girls Want to Know About Boys." (See pp. 37–40.)

If you find yourself continually arguing with your girlfriend about what the two of you will do on a given day, perhaps Deena's idea is right. You could compromise. One day you could do what you want, another day you could do what she wants. You may discover that you like each other's choices, or you may just have to grin and bear it. Either way, both of you will be happy at least fifty percent of the time, and you'll do a lot less arguing.

– WHY DO GIRLS TRY TO BOSS YOU AROUND IN FRONT OF THEIR FRIENDS? –

Girls complain that guys behave differently in front of their friends. They say you start acting crazy and making stupid jokes; they claim that you are not as affectionate toward them when you're around your friends. But boys tell me that girls also put on a different face in front of *their* friends. What girls do is try to boss their boyfriends around. Here's why.

> To make myself look like Miss Hot Shot!
> *Nicole, 16*

> To show I have him in check.
> *Monique, 17*

> I want my friends to know that I have him in the palm of my hand and that he is scared of me.
> *Marion, 16*

> I don't want them to think I'm his slave.
> *Carol, 16*

A lot has been said about guys being "macho." Do you recognize the female equivalent here? Women like to show that they're in control just as much as men do. *Vedral's Believe It or Not*: In their own way, women are just as macho as men are—or "femacho," to coin a word.

– WHY DO GIRLS TRY TO GET EVEN WHENEVER YOU DO SOMETHING WRONG? –

If you go out with your friends one evening instead of seeing your girlfriend, she may do the same thing to you the next night. If you forget to call her one night, she'll probably do the same thing to you one day next week, and so on. Why?

> To give him a taste of his own medicine.
> *Ro, 16*

> I want him to feel the put-down the way I felt it the night before.
> *Allison, 15*

> Who the hell is he? Shall I walk around on tiptoes just so as not to disturb his train of thought?
> *Jennifer, 15*

> I say to myself, I'll fix his behind—and I do.
> *Fabaya, 16*

> You've got to show him that his thinking is all wrong. It's not fair that when he goes out with his friends it's fine, but when you go out with your friends all hell breaks loose.
> *Barbara, 16*

Girls don't want you to "get out of hand." They're afraid that if they let you get away with too much, you may walk all over them. Are they right? If you're honest, I'll bet you'll admit that you're glad your girlfriend stands up for her rights.

– WHY DO GIRLS NAG? –

Lots of fighting between guys and their girlfriends is the result of nagging. Does your girlfriend nag you? What do girls nag their boyfriends about and why do they do it?

> I nag because he smokes weed, and I don't want to be associated with a loser.
>
> *Holly, 17*

> I nag him about wearing cologne. I like a guy to smell nice.
>
> *Adriana, 16*

> I nag him about coming on time. It's annoying to be ready and have to sit in your room for a half an hour.
>
> *Dominica, 16*

> I nag him about finishing school and getting a job. I want him to have a future.
>
> *Maria, 17*

> I nag about his playing basketball so much. That's all he ever does. Play basketball.
>
> *Annie, 16*

Notice the clear admission: "I nag because..." They don't seem to be ashamed of the fact that they nag.

They do it for a reason—because they want you to look better and be better—just as concerned parents nag their children, and husbands and wives nag each other. It may be annoying, but it's really a compliment. If she didn't care, would she nag?

In addition, nagging is one of the attributes associated with women. Traditionally, it has been their job to keep the family on track, so they may tend to nag a little more than men do. (There are exceptions, of course. Some men could nag a woman into an asylum.)

– WHY ARE GIRLS MOODY? –

A sudden change of mood, from happy and optimistic to sullen and pessimistic, can cause an argument. Boys claim that girls have these "mood swings" quite often, and they wonder why.

> Probably because he did something to me to make me unhappy. Maybe he yelled at me about something or said something mean about the way I looked.
>
> *Diane, 18*

> He usually does something unintentionally that really turns me off or depresses me.
>
> *Eileen, 15*

> It depends on the way he's acting. My mood reflects his.
>
> *Ally, 15*

> If he starts joking and kidding around like a moron, I change moods.
>
> *Jenny, 16*

Maybe he talks about something or someone I don't like.

Dawn, 16

In spite of what you may have heard, women don't just change moods for no reason. There is *always* a reason and, as you now know, that reason is often related to *you*. You probably did or said something to upset her. But often girls won't come out and tell you what's on their minds. They think that if you care about them, you'll be able to figure it out or you'll ask. I admit it's not really fair to expect a boy to be able to guess. But girls do. So the next time you notice a "mood swing" in your girlfriend, analyze the situation. What did you just say or do? If you still can't figure out what happened, then tell her you know there's something wrong but you don't know what it is, and then ask her why she's not happy. If you say this in a kind rather than belligerent (warlike) manner, she'll tell you why and you'll have avoided an argument.

– WHY DO GIRLS TAKE THEIR FRUSTRATIONS OUT ON THEIR BOYFRIENDS? –

Sometimes a girl will take out her anger on her boyfriend, even if he is not the cause of that anger. Why do they do this? Girls admit:

Because he's available.

Diane, 19

I don't really mean to, it's just that he's there and I have to take it out on someone.

Tanya, 16

Because he keeps saying, "What's wrong with you," until I yell at *him*.

Maxine, 17

He's like a best friend. I know he'll realize it's not him. I trust him.

Jemara, 16

Most girls don't think of their boyfriends as just a boyfriend. They think of him as a friend—someone they can trust and confide in, complain or even cry to. They hope you will care enough to understand. If your girlfriend seems upset and isn't acting right, the *worst* thing you can do is to say something like: "What's the matter with *you*, something bugging you and you're taking it out on *me*?"

The best thing you can do is to say something like: "What happened? I can tell there's something on your mind," and then listen sympathetically to whatever she says, showing her that you care about her feelings enough to overlook the way she's behaving. Then, instead of turning against you, she'll radiate love toward you—because she'll think of you as being on *her* side!

In conclusion, arguments between girlfriends and boyfriends are normal, and will continue to take place until the end of time. The goal is not to stop them from happening, but to prevent them from exploding into all-out wars. Sometimes, if you can take a step backward and look at the big picture, asking yourself "What's really going on here?" then you can be calm enough to talk about it instead of breaking up. If you care about the relationship, this is a good technique to use to save it.

4

Girls' Attitudes About Spending—Your Time and Your Money

When it comes to what girls expect you to do with your time and money, things haven't changed much at all. They would like you to spend a lot of both on them—and to like it, too! The latter is very important to them. If you don't have the right attitude, you might as well not bother. No girl likes to think her boyfriend spends time and money on her only because she forces him to. On the other hand, no matter how much time or money you spend on your girlfriend, chances are, she still thinks it's not enough. To understand why this is so, you need to look below the surface to see what messages your girlfriend thinks you are sending by the way you share time and money with her. Both time and money are very symbolic and your girlfriend probably reads something into them whether or not it's really there.

– WHY DO GIRLS THINK YOU SHOULD SPEND LOTS OF MONEY ON THEM? –

Boys continually ask this question. They would like to know what goes on in girls' minds concerning the issue of their boyfriends spending money on them. Exactly what does your spending money mean to a girl?

> That's my style. I love being treated like a queen or a goddess.
>
> *Marthe, 15*

> He doesn't have to buy me a lot; a little will do just fine. He owes it to me for being there for him.
>
> *Irene, 15*

> It feels good to get things from someone you love. If he leaves, at least you'll have things to remind you of him.
>
> *Beth, 17*

> I like going to fine places—not McDonald's and Kentucky Fried Chicken. I want Red Lobster or Sizzler. I demand that a guy go all-out to please me—to make the evening go well. That tells me I mean a lot to him.
>
> *Dawn, 17*

> It makes me feel cared for. I like to be pampered by a guy.
>
> *Spanky, 18*

> It proves that he loves me. If he didn't, why would he be spending his money on me?
>
> *Tanya, 16*

Some girls feel that spending money on them is a sign of respect. It makes them feel important—like a queen or a goddess. Others believe it's proof that you really care.

"But I can't afford it," you may think. Yes you can. As Irene says, it doesn't have to be something very expensive. Look for opportunities to give your girl a token of your affection. You can find little ways to make her feel appreciated. Then when you get a good job and can afford to spend money, you can go out with girls like seventeen-year-old Dawn who expects to be taken out in style. Guys she dates are probably two years older than she is, and most likely can afford her tastes. On the other hand, you may decide you want a girl who's offbeat enough to be able to see that dinner in an out-of-the-way diner may be just as romantic a gesture as a Red Lobster or Sizzler.

– HE WOULD RATHER WASTE TIME WITH HIS FRIENDS THAN BE WITH ME –

One of the biggest causes of disagreements between boys and girls, and often between men and women, is the question of how much time to spend together. Girls seem to think that their boyfriends should spend a lot more time with them than they do, because when I asked them, "Why do you think that your boyfriend doesn't spend enough time with you," all of the girls had answers like the following:

> Because they don't. Some of them would rather waste time with their friends than be with you, and when you ask them to come over, they take their time getting there.
>
> *Truly, 17*

Every weekend he wants to go to a party or to a movie with his friends.

Diane, 16

If you really love someone, you'd like to spend as much time as possible together. If he doesn't want it that way, you'll know there is a problem somewhere.

Sonia, 15

I complain because I like him so much I want to spend all the time possible with him.

Lorita, 14

Girls don't seem to understand that guys don't have as great a need for an in-depth emotional connection as they do. I tried to help you gentlemen out on this problem by explaining to girls (see Chapter 4 of the other half of this book, "What Girls Want to Know About Boys") why it is that a lot of you would rather hang out with the guys—based on what you told me and what I know from psychology and personal observation. But this is one of those problems that isn't going to go away. It may lessen as you grow older and find yourselves more eager to make a deep commitment to someone, but the fact remains that girls are just more romantic than boys and have different ideas on how to spend time.

In addition, as mentioned before, our society has always encouraged women to build their lives around a man. While this is beginning to change, and women are becoming more independent, most girls are still geared toward investing too much of themselves in their boyfriends. Your girlfriend probably doesn't realize that not only is this not good for her (it keeps her from achieving personal goals, etc.), but it is not good for you or your relationship with her because it makes you feel smothered and trapped.

What should you do if you find yourself arguing with your girl about not spending enough time with her? Tell her you really enjoy her company but you also need time for friends and other interests, and encourage her to do the same. The only trouble with this idea is, you may be like so many guys I've met: They don't want their girlfriends to have too many outside interests—they see that as a threat. Well, if this is you, don't complain when you end up with a clinging vine. But if you really want an independent woman, you have to expect that she'll go places and see people without you. Independent women don't stay at home hoping the phone will ring while you're out shooting pool with the guys.

– WHY ARE GIRLS JEALOUS OF YOUR FRIENDS? –

Even when you *are* spending time with your girlfriend, trouble can arise if you don't give her your full attention. For example, you may have noticed that your girlfriend gets upset if you're with her and you leave her for a while to talk to your friends. Why do girls feel this way?

> I feel rejected. If he's with me, his friends could wait.
>
> *Sue-Ellen, 14*

> It makes me feel that his friends are more important than I am.
>
> *Rosie, 16*

> If you're not with him a lot, you'd like it to be only you and him for that little time you have

together—and you get furious if you lose any of it.

Allison, 15

I feel left out—like I can't get in on the conversation. I want to be in on the fun, too!

Natalie, 16

Girls usually need more private time with a guy than a guy needs with a girl. When they finally get to be alone with you, they don't appreciate any interruption. It feels like an invasion to them—an abrupt intrusion into the atmosphere that they have created with you. Think of it this way: How do you feel when you're talking to a girl you just met—trying to get her interested in you—and your friend comes along and interrupts with some story or joke? You want to tell him to get the hell out of there, right? Well, many girls feel this way all the time when they're with you even though they already have you as a boyfriend. Girls are just more interested in intimate relationships than guys are.

If you find your girlfriend getting upset when you leave her to talk to your friends, instead of arguing with her, see it from her point of view and try saying something like: "I'm sorry I was talking with ——— so long. It was rude of me to keep you waiting..." She'll appreciate your understanding attitude so much that she'll probably say something like: "Oh, that's all right. I didn't mind at all"—and she'll mean it, too, because you were sensitive to her feelings.

– IF HE REALLY CARED HE WOULD AT LEAST CALL –

Why are girls so insecure about their relationships with guys? What makes them think "it's over" just because a guy doesn't call or come around for a few days? Girls are quick to answer:

> If he really cared, he would at least call and say he's been busy.
>
> *Lola, 17*

> Because he obviously wasn't so eager to see me. If he didn't care enough to make the effort, then he's not worth my time.
>
> *Marthe, 15*

> I feel like a fool sitting there waiting for him to call while he's probably having a good time with his friends—without me. That makes me furious.
>
> *Florence, 17*

> I want to be first in my boyfriend's life. If he doesn't even call me for a few days, I feel like I'm not first anymore.
>
> *Dorothy, 17*

> I'm insecure about the relationship.
>
> *Cyndi, 18*

> You start thinking about the arguments and fights you had and you think maybe he wants to break up with you.
>
> *Rosemary, 16*

When you don't call a girl for a few days, she goes through three stages. First, she's hurt because she thinks she's not as important to you as she used to be. Then she becomes angry. "How dare he insult me this way?" she thinks, as she imagines you having fun with all of your friends—not even thinking of her while she sits waiting by the phone. Finally, she starts to imagine things, often ending with the thought that you might be planning to break up with her. It usually doesn't occur to a girl that she may be on your mind constantly, but you were just too busy to call—or you didn't feel like calling, and you assumed she would understand. Most girls don't put their feelings for you on hold while they're busy with other things. Don't make the mistake of expecting them to understand that you do and that a temporary lack of attention from you is not a sign of something wrong. They never will. Their minds just don't work that way.

So, if you don't want to lose your girlfriend, think about it from her point of view. It's worth the small amount of effort. If you take her for granted once too often, another guy who understands women will come along and before you know it, your girlfriend will be *gone*, and you'll be left saying "What did I do wrong?" —all for lack of an occasional five-minute phone call to say "I'm thinking about you even though I'm not with you."

No one is telling you to become a slave to your girlfriend. All it takes is a little consideration, and instead of losing your girlfriend, *you* can be the guy who gets the lovely girls who are neglected by *their* boyfriends.

5

How Girls Really Feel About Sex

Do teenage girls enjoy sexual intercourse, or do they just pretend to? If they don't really enjoy it, why do they do it? Why do most girls assume that a guy is "out for one thing only," even when he's not? Why do girls prance around in fine clothing and act sexy in front of guys, and then refuse to have sex? Are they just teasing? These are some of the sex-related questions that will be answered in this chapter.

– WHY DO GIRLS ASSUME A GUY IS "OUT FOR JUST ONE THING"? –

This is a favorite question asked by teenage boys, plenty of whom *are* sincere about trying to develop a relationship with a girl. But lots of girls don't see it that way.

> You *never* find a guy that just wants to build a good relationship. They always want something

out of it. They'll be nice for a while and then they get you in your house alone and it turns out they want a return for their kindness.

Dawn, 16

I never thought that way, but I learned. When a guy approaches with a stupid look and he starts with the basic questions...he's only after one thing—and it isn't a relationship.

Lila, 17

Because more than one guy has tried the same line on me and now I'm suspicious.

Nina, 16

Sex is always on their minds.

Lisa, 19

I was conditioned by my parents that all guys want is one thing, especially if they're nice to you.

Danielle, 16

Don't feel too bad, guys. Some girls are willing to give you a very slight benefit of the doubt:

The vast majority are out for one thing. The other guys are one in a million.

Jennifer, 15

Not all guys are out for one thing, but most are, especially if you're pretty. So you have to keep your guard up or you'll get hurt.

Simone, 16

Most of the guys are just out for "that," and I really do give credit to the guys that aren't.

Maria, 16

> If a guy is nice to me and doesn't try anything for a long time, then I know he's really interested in a relationship.
>
> *Trina, 15*

According to girls, most guys are "guilty as charged." How do you plead? If you don't want to be thought of as a guy who's "out for one thing only," take Trina's advice and "don't try anything for a long time." During that time the girl can get to know you well enough to see that you care about something besides getting her into bed with you. (And that's the biggest turn-on of all for a girl.)

– "JUST BECAUSE I LOOK GOOD DOESN'T MEAN I'M FOR SALE" –

Some guys say it's really the girls' fault that they put the make on them, because why else would girls dress and act so sexy if they didn't want "it"? Boys want girls to answer this question: "If you're not interested in sex, why do you prance around in fine clothing and show off all your assets to get us excited?" Girls become quite annoyed when they answer this question.

> Just because I look good doesn't mean they shouldn't be able to control themselves. Why should they be such animals? They ought to try having some respect for girls.
>
> *Marthe, 15*

> If I go out looking nice, it's not because I'm looking for sex.
>
> *Allison, 16*

Just because I look good doesn't mean I'm for sale. Look but don't touch.

Jenny, 15

All I want is attention—maybe a little cuddling. Why must sex be a goal?

Liza, 17

Most girls like to have nice clothing but are not ready for sex yet. They want the guy's attention, and when the guy misses the point and tries something, the girl is disgusted with him.

Mona, 16

Girls want to look good, but they don't see why that's any reason for you not to behave like gentlemen. Their reaction is: How dare you assume that you have a right to "attack" just because they dress beautifully and behave coquettishly? They want you to admire them, not manhandle them. That's the only signal they intend to send when they dress up.

– DO GIRLS ENJOY SEX? –

It's common knowledge that teenage boys hit their sexual peak at around nineteen. That is, on a scale of one to ten, the sexual urge of teenage boys, fifteen to nineteen years of age, rates somewhere between an eight and a ten. To be blunt about it, you are very, very "horny"—driven by your hormones. Girls, on the other hand, hit their sexual peak in their thirties. So as teenagers, they have a sexual desire rating that is very low, probably between a one and a three. They are not as driven by their hormones and are therefore not nearly as "horny" as you are—as you might have noticed. And when they do have sex, they don't usually enjoy it very much. Here's what the girls say:

> To tell you the truth, it's not all that great. I wonder why people make such a big deal of it. I think there might be something wrong with me sometimes.
>
> *Corina, 16*

> Enjoy it? Hell, no. I can't wait until it's over. In fact, half the time I wonder why in the world he's getting so worked up. I say to myself, "Am I missing something here?"
>
> *Susan, 16*

> I don't really enjoy it, but I like having sex with him because it makes me feel close to him. I mean as far as it being the ultimate thrill—no. But as far as feeling that he really loves me at that moment, yes.
>
> *Nancy, 15*

"Oh, really," you might be saying. "Then why do so many girls have sex with guys?" Girls give in for a lot of reasons. They fall in love with you and want to please you; they enjoy the love part of sex—the hugging, kissing, touching, and cuddling. They love the closeness and affection of it all. But sexual intercourse is *not* what their bodies are looking for.

Many girls love the "love" part so much that they may seem to be teasing you, leading you on. They don't really want to have sex at all—they just want all the stuff that leads up to it—the preliminaries. But things get too hot to handle and then they feel obligated to "follow through" because you get so worked up. If they do try to stop you, you start spouting lines like, "I love you, I must have you. . . ."

Now can you understand why a girl becomes furious

when you try to break up with her after having said "I love you" just to get her into bed?

– WHY DO GIRLS PRETEND TO ENJOY SEX EVEN WHEN THEY DON'T? –

Although most girls don't really enjoy sex at such a young age, they often try to fool you into believing that they're having a good time. Here's why they do it:

> I don't want to hurt his feelings after he's tried so hard to please me.
>
> *Nancy, 17*

> I don't want him to think there's something wrong with me—that I'm not into it... you know, like I'm not sexy.
>
> *Corina, 16*

> I'm afraid I'll lose him if I don't have sex with him, so I keep up the act.
>
> *Susan, 16*

> To get it over with quickly.
>
> *Jo-Anne, 17*

Right now you may be saying to yourself: "This lady doesn't know what she's talking about... I don't know what kind of girls she's been talking to... I've been with girls who..." Yes, you're right to challenge me. Of course, there are exceptions. Some girls (very few) do have a high sex drive at an early age. Maybe you've met one of them. Lucky you! But before you become too pleased with yourself, listen to this. There are girls who use sex as a substitute for love. They *seem* to love *sex*. They can't get enough of it because for the time they're engaging in sexual intercourse they feel needed and loved. What passes off as a high sex drive, then, may very well be the sad fact that your "sex maniac" is starved for the love she never got from her parents.

– HOW DO GIRLS FEEL ABOUT A GUY WHO HAS A REPUTATION AS A "STUD"? –

We all know how guys feel about *girls* who jump into any available bed. Such girls are called sluts, freaks, whores, and the like. But how do girls feel about guys with a reputation for having sex with a lot of girls? You probably think that they're impressed. But girls say:

> I say he's easy. He's a slut. Who wants a guy who's most likely to get every disease in the book?
>
> *Laurie, 17*

> I think that guys like that are insecure and they don't have a good self-image so they need to sleep around to make themselves feel like a man. They also probably have AIDS.
>
> *Marthe, 15*

> I think they are the dirt of the earth and should be put out of their misery.
>
> *Jana, 16*

> I'd feel like a "numba" with one of those guys. No way I'd ever go to bed with one of them.
>
> *Cyndi, 18*

> I do not have respect for them. He wears a mask of "macho."
>
> *Leah, 16*

> I would be afraid to go out with him because people would assume I was doing things with him even if I wasn't.
>
> *Tracy, 16*

Guys who have a reputation for many sexual conquests may be the envy of their male friends, but as you can see, girls think of them as "sluts," disease-ridden, insecure losers. It's not a good idea for a guy to have a lot of sexual conquests, but it's even worse if you brag about them. It causes girls to avoid you like the plague, because today there is a very real plague going around—AIDS. And so-called safe sex or not, most girls are not going to be stupid enough to take a chance with a "run-around" boy.

– AREN'T GIRLS AFRAID GUYS WILL "KISS AND TELL"? –

Guys wonder as much about why girls will have sex with them as about why they won't. One of the questions a lot of you were curious about was why girls have sex when they know that the guy might spread the word about her. Girls say:

> You don't think about it at the time. Maybe you're high and before you know it, you do something dumb and you regret it the next morning.
>
> *Pat, 16*

> I do it because I believe him when he says that only immature boys talk about their sex life.
>
> *Lois, 17*

That's why I would never have sex with a guy who lives in my neighborhood.

Brenda, 16

That would never happen to me. I'm extremely choosy, and the only guys I've been with would never do anything like that. Who needs a bad reputation?

Lisa, 17

The girl is either not really worrying about the consequences (high), is too trusting ("I believe him"), or she thinks she's smart enough to pick a guy who can't hurt her reputation (because he doesn't know anyone she knows) or won't ("They never do anything like that"). In short, girls take a chance on a guy or they engage in "magical" thinking. (Magical thinking is when people believe something won't happen just because they don't want it to happen.)

– WHY DO SOME GIRLS "KISS AND TELL"? –

Boys are not the only ones who are sometimes guilty of "kiss and tell." Girls do it, too, and boys find this very hard to understand. "Why do some girls talk about their sexual experiences and even brag about them to their girlfriends?" the boys ask. Most of the girls who answered claim to be talking about why *other* girls "kiss and tell."

It's just immaturity. They're trying to show that they're experienced.

Gloria, 17

Deep down they're ashamed and they're trying to make it okay.

Jeannie, 15

I talk about it because I want to tell my friends and see if they had the same experience, too.

Deena, 17

They talk about it so that you will start telling that you had sex, too.

Rosemary, 16

It doesn't seem that girls really "brag" about their sexual experiences. But they do talk about them because they seem to need to confide in someone. Maybe this is because, for girls, sex is still more of a taboo, a forbidden act, so that once a girl has "crossed the line" into sex, she needs to sort things out. Also, she needs "allies"— other girls who have had the same experience and can make her feel as if she's not the only one. What may seem like bragging may actually be an effort to cope with mixed emotions: guilt, fear, anxiety, pregnancy worries, awakening pleasure, etc.

– DO GIRLS EXPECT ME TO BE RESPONSIBLE FOR BIRTH CONTROL? –

We'll end this chapter the way many sexual encounters end: with pregnancy. Boys want to know if girls would blame their boyfriend if they got pregnant. Here's what girls say:

He is just as much to blame as I am. I can't get pregnant by myself, you know!

Jennifer, 15

At first I would blame myself for being so stupid, but then I would blame him, too, because he is just as much a part of it as I am. I would ask him, "What do we do now?" You better believe I wouldn't think it was just my problem.

Ada, 15

It's true that the girl, if she's smart, should think about protection before she gets in the bed, not after she bakes the bread, because if she does get pregnant, the guy could always just run away to the other side of the world and then what?

Nicky, 16

I would blame him because I'm not the type of girl who throws herself at a guy. If I got pregnant, it would be because he had pressured me into sex. So since he's making all the moves, I feel he should be the one using protection—*if* I give in, and that's a big if.

Ro, 17

Although it's true that it's the girl and not you who will actually get pregnant and carry the baby for nine months, you'd better be *very* concerned about protection. If a girl becomes pregnant and chooses to have the baby, even if you're callous enough to walk away and never see the child, the courts will force you to pay child support until the child is twenty-one years old. This means you'll be working and hustling when you should be finishing school and enjoying your youth.

Everybody has to pay his or her dues. Guys don't *really* get away with anything. My advice to you is: Don't take chances. If you have intercourse with a girl, assume total responsibility for the consequences—then there can be no problem.

I would love to end this chapter with a sermon on sexual morality. I would say things like "You should not

- 148 -

have sex at an early age—just because you're a boy. You can and should control yourself." (As you know—see pp. 54-55 on the subject of guys and self-control.) I would talk about how wrong it is to "use" a girl just for sex, and on and on and on. But I won't do that. I respect your intelligence. It's time for you to put together what you've read here, what you've been taught at home and/or in your place of worship, and what you've found out for yourself in life. Just remember one thing: Whatever you do eventually returns to you. It's like planting a farm. Nothing happens overnight, but the seeds you planted grow—and you get exactly what you planted. If you use people, behave recklessly, and discount the wisdom of your parents and teachers, problems will eventually crop up as a result. If, on the other hand, you are considerate, treat girls the way you would wish to be treated if you were a girl, and are true to the values you know deep down in your heart are the right ones, then your life will "bloom"—romantically, sexually, and in every other way.

6

I Can Never Figure Out Why Girls... (Strange Ways of Girls)

Do some of the things girls say and do puzzle you? A lot of these things are trivial, but guys I talked to all seemed to want to know how girls would explain them. For example, do you wonder why girls take two hours to get dressed when it takes you about thirty minutes? Why even the most beautiful and shapely girls call themselves "ugly" and "fat"? Why a girl will tell a guy to get lost even though she really likes him? Why so many girls go for older guys? These are some of the questions that will be discussed in this chapter.

– WHY DO GIRLS TAKE SO LONG TO GET DRESSED? –

One of the main things that puzzle boys about girls is why they care so much about their looks. Their hair, makeup, clothing, and shape seem to worry them just about twenty-four hours a day. True, boys also worry about their clothing, hair, and physical appearance, but not the way girls do. It's easy to figure out why. Ever since the beginning of time, it has been the role of the female to dress up and strut her stuff in front of the male in order to attract his attention. The female "vanity" attitude is equal to the male "macho" attitude. Just the way a guy feels he has to make sure he appears strong, hard, and courageous, a girl has to make sure she appears feminine, sensual, and attractive. But a guy does not put on the "macho" act just for girls. He's also trying to impress his friends. Girls do the same thing. When a girl gets dressed, she pictures how other girls will be dressed and she attempts to make herself look better than her "competition." She is also aware of how critical she is of how other girls dress, so she tries very hard to avoid the faults she often sees in other girls' dress styles. Girls also enjoy being complimented by other girls. Their goal is to be the envy of the most popular and well-dressed girls.

I asked girls why they take two hours to get dressed. They say:

It takes me forever to find something to wear. Then I have to spend time on my hair. I have to wash, dry, tease, and comb it.

Dolly, 17

I always find something wrong. Either my clothes get lint on them or my hair doesn't go the way I really want it. I've got to find stockings without runs, find the right shoes to match the outfit, and then do my makeup. If my makeup isn't right, I'll wash it all off and start over.

Dawn, 16

First, I take a shower to really be clean and smelling nice. Then as I get dressed, I listen to music. I get interrupted by the phone and start laughing and joking with my friends.

Christy, 15

It takes me two hours because I want to impress my boyfriend. I don't want people to tell him that he has an ugly girlfriend.

Annie, 16

Whether guys admit it or not, they respect a girl who puts effort into her appearance. Who wants a girlfriend who rolls out of bed looking and smelling like a pig.

Amber, 14

I take a long time because I don't want those other girls to outdress me or to think I don't look as good or better than they do. Girls notice things that even boys don't notice. When you're getting dressed, you keep that in mind.

Rhonda, 15

– WHY DO GIRLS WORRY SO MUCH ABOUT THEIR HAIR? –

Girls are always complaining about their hair. Most girls will refuse to leave the house until they think their hair looks absolutely perfect, and if, on a particular occasion, they're forced to go out feeling that it doesn't look right, they suffer all day. Why?

They say a woman's beauty is found in her hair. It's the hair that attracts the most attention.

Truly, 17

That's part of my personality. The way my hair looks shows the way I feel about myself.

Monique, 17

It's an important accessory to the overall look. If your hair look goods, *you* look good.

Crystal, 17

If your hair is all matted, people think you're a dirtbag. Also because of other girls. I don't want anyone to have cooler hair than me.

Theresa, 15

I like to make a striking impression on everyone I meet. I want everyone to walk away saying, "God, she's gorgeous." That's just me.

Bridgette, 16

As you can see, to a girl, her hair is like a crown or a mane. She counts on it to attract guys. If a girl's hair appears beautiful to her when she looks in the mirror, she leaves the house with confidence. She walks out thinking: "I look great. I'm going to have a good time." But if it doesn't, she can feel like a loser and act defensive all day long.

– WHY GIRLS GET UPSET WHEN YOU JOKE ABOUT THEIR APPEARANCE –

The worst thing you can do to a girl is to crack a joke about the way she looks. Most guys think it's funny to make comments about a girl's hair, makeup, or clothing. They like to tease girls—they use it as a way to start up a conversation. But girls take teasing seriously. It usually cuts them like a knife. Your words stay with them, and they keep asking themselves: "Do I really look that bad?" Girls say:

> Being teased makes me build up a complex. I start feeling ugly and wondering if guys talk to me out of pity.
>
> *Margie, 17*

> They make me feel like I'm not good enough for them.
>
> *Cheryl, 15*

> My ex-boyfriend always joked around about my height, which I'm really sensitive about because I'm short. I'd get furious because he should know better than to tease me about something that he knows bothers me so much. If he really loved me, he wouldn't do that to me.
>
> *Mona, 16*

> I'm small-chested, so when a guy jokes about my shape, I want to hide.
>
> *Cynthia, 18*

> I get upset because I know I'm fat and I don't like hearing the truth.
>
> *Ada, 16*

> Because usually when people joke around, in the back of their minds they mean it seriously.
>
> *Jackie, 15*

> I start wondering if maybe they're right and I really do look that bad.
>
> *Tammie, 16*

Mona knows she is short, Cynthia is self-conscious about being flat-chested, and poor Ada envies other girls who are not fat. The fact is, girls are so self-conscious about their appearance that you can't tell them anything they don't know about themselves. The difference is, you may think their "flaw" is cute—maybe you like small breasts or girls who are petite—but they never do. Or maybe it's just not a big deal to you whether your girl should lose a little weight, so you think it's fun to tease. But it's a huge deal to her, and not only does she find it hard to believe you could like her with such a flaw, but now you're telling the whole world about it. It's as if you put a big sign over their heads for everyone to stare at: SHORT MONA, FLAT-CHESTED CYNTHIA, or FAT ADA.

Up until now, you may not have realized how painful it is for girls when you tease them about their appearance. Now that you know, I suggest that instead of teasing them, you give them some well-thought-out compliments. Girls are starving for honest compliments, and if you're one of the few observant, sensitive guys who knows how to give them, a girl will fall in love with you. (See Bibliography for *I Dare You*, a whole book on this subject.)

– WHY GIRLS CALL THEMSELVES UGLY AND FAT WHEN THEY'RE NOT –

If you need added proof that girls are starving for honest compliments, notice that even the prettiest and shapeliest girls are always calling themselves ugly and fat. That's because they're hoping that you'll protest—tell them it's not true—that they're pretty and sexy. No matter how pretty they are, they are still worried that they are not good enough. Why is it so important to them for you to reassure them about their looks? Girls answer the question:

When a girl looks in the mirror, she sees herself as unattractive. When a boy looks in the mirror, he sees himself as a gorgeous stud.

Lisa, 17

I'm really not satisfied with my body, but if he tells me he thinks it's great, then I figure either it's not really so bad or else he really loves me—and either way I feel a lot better.

Jenny, 15

I guess it's because when I was ten to thirteen I was really heavy, and people use to laugh and make fun of me, so now, even though I'm thin, I'm not confident about my appearance.

Diane, 19

Because everyone has faults, and when you're pretty, you tend to exaggerate your faults. You get depressed when you realize you are not perfect.

Eileen, 16

Insecurity. Because I know there's always a girl with a better shape and a prettier face.

Jennifer, 15

When I say I'm fat, I want him to say, "No you're not. You're beautiful." I just need to hear the words sometimes.

Sandy, 18

Most men eventually learn to compliment women instead of putting them down. The few fools who don't find themselves alone a lot of the time. The only kind of woman who would stay around a man who continually "jokes" about her appearance (which is really a put-down, especially if it comes from an adult, who should know better) is a woman with very low self-esteem. She believes in her heart that she isn't worthy of better treatment, so she stays with him.

Teasing is normal for most boys, but if you learn early to turn your teasing into complimenting, you'll be that much ahead of the game. You'll be considered to be mature and girls will want to be around *you*—even if you're not the best-looking guy on the block.

– WHY GIRLS TELL YOU TO GO AWAY WHEN THEY REALLY LIKE YOU –

Are they embarrassed because they think you can read their minds and that you know how "eager" they are to be with you? Are they nervous? Are they testing you to see how much you like them and if you are willing to pursue them? Are they afraid of the strong attraction they feel for you because they have been hurt before, so they run? The answer is yes to all of the above.

> I don't want him to think I like him. Not just yet.
> *Truly, 17*

> Why give him the satisfaction of thinking he can have me the first couple of times he talks to me?
> *Laurette, 16*

> So he won't think I'm easy. If they think you're hard to get, they'll appreciate you more.
> *Dara, 16*

> I get nervous when I get around him because I like him too much, so I'll be nice to all the other guys that I don't like, but to him I'll put on an act and make believe I don't care about him at all. I guess

it's because I'm afraid if he knows how I feel he might laugh at me and say he doesn't feel the same way.

Fabaya, 17

To see if he really likes me. If he really wants me, he'll keep trying.

Ellen, 16

I've been hurt by someone before and I don't want to give anyone the advantage over me.

Marion, 16

If a girl gives you a hard time when you're trying to get to know her, don't let it throw you. Girls are conditioned to believe that they're supposed to play "hard to get." In addition, they are often afraid to expose their feelings for fear of rejection, so they put on an act, pretending not to care for the boy they really like the most. Don't let them know *you* know what they're up to, but keep on pursuing them. After they prove their point, chances are they'll come around—especially if you make use of some of the tips in this book. If you want to find out some of the ways to girl's heart, read the next section on older guys—because they know.

– WHY GIRLS LIKE OLDER GUYS –

Guys complain that it isn't fair that most girls refuse to go out with guys their own age. They want to date older guys. Why? Here's what girls say...

They have more experience and they treat you with respect.

Malissa, 16

They're more sensitive and understandng.
Michelle, 17

They know more about life and they know how to make a girl feel special and wanted. They're not afraid to give a girl a compliment once in a while.
Margie, 16

I find them more exciting.
Lois, 15

He acts like a man, not a child, so you feel like a lady and not like a teen.
Lilly, 16

Guys my age are very immature. Mentally and physically.
Marthe, 15

Because it makes *me* feel older. Just imagine me going out with a guy my own age—their idea of a good time is hanging out with the guys on the street corner, and their idea of getting to know a girl is pulling her hair or telling her she's got ketchup on her dress. Very funny.
Patty, 14

What can you do, boys? Be everything the older guys seem to be to these girls, treat a girl with respect. Be sensitive and understanding. Make her feel special. Act like a man and not like a child. But if all that doesn't work, go out with a girl who's two years younger than you.

If you want to make your life with girls run more smoothly, it pays to try to understand them. What's the use of saying, "Too bad. I'm not going to change the way I act just to please them." Let's face it, guys, if you have a goal, isn't it intelligent to find out the best way to achieve it? If you want to get the girls you like to go out with you, then why not do what's necessary to get them?

By understanding girls' ways and using basic psychology, you'll find yourself less frustrated and less rejected. In fact, you'll be surprised to see that girls you couldn't attract before now come straight to *you*.

7

What Turns a Girl Off? What Turns a Girl On?

It's easy to turn girls off. All it takes is the wrong language, attitude, or clothes. On the other hand, it's just as easy to turn girls on—if you know what to do. In this chapter, girls give away their secrets—they tell you exactly what makes them reject a guy and precisely what causes them to wish a guy were *their* boyfriend. Let's get the turn-offs out of the way first so that we can end on a positive note with the turn-ons.

You can drive girls away from you by the way you behave, the way you talk, or the way you look.

– BEHAVIOR TURN-OFFS –

If you want a girl to cut you off cold, all you have to do is act like any of the following:

> A hard-up sex-hungry pig. He would be out the door before he came in.
>
> *Marthe, 15*

A guy that tries to impress you with his gold jewelry, cars, and money.

Diane, 16

A guy who thinks he's God's gift to women. Guys who think they're God's gift should take another hard look at themselves.

Kim, 15

If a guy is stupid in front of his friends, or if he doesn't know how to approach a girl when his friends are watching him, even if he's really gorgeous, I wouldn't go out with him.

Lilly, 17

Girls hate guys who are too "obvious." If a guy acts as if he's desperate (sexually), a girl will walk the other way. Girls like a guy to show restraint and respect. If he doesn't, as Marthe says: "He would be out the door before he came in."

Unfortunately, some guys don't believe they're good enough to attract girls by just being themselves, so they try to impress girls with their possessions. But girls don't like guys to be "obvious" about their possessions, because they see through you and think you are immature or worse (insecure—they think that you believe you're unable to attract a girl's attention without them). There's nothing wrong with having gold jewelry, money, or a fine car, but you have to act as if they mean nothing to you. Don't talk about them all the time. A girl isn't blind—she'll see that you have them. Once you open your mouth to talk about them yourself, you blow the entire effect of having them. No one could fault you for having them. But girls think bragging is really not cool.

Girls can't stand conceited guys. If you act as if you think you're "God's gift to the world," a girl will avoid you because she'll say to herself, "All this guy wants is to be admired. He's all caught up in himself. I can forget about getting any attention from him." A girl likes a guy who thinks *she* is God's gift to the world, a guy who makes *her* feel like a queen.

Girls are turned off by a guy who acts stupid toward a girl just because his friends are watching. They can tell if you're putting on an act just to impress your friends. If you like a girl and you want to approach her, concentrate on the way you think the girl would like you to behave. Don't worry about what your friends think. After all, you already *have* your friends. It's the girl you're trying to attract.

– VERBAL TURN-OFFS –

Words are really symbols of thought. When you talk to a girl, you're showing her what your mind contains. No wonder girls run when they think your mind is filled with nothing but "rap talk," yourself, or foul language. Girls can't stand:

> A guy who comes up to me and says: "Yo, baby, I wish you were my girl," and "yo, baby" this and "yo, baby" that... It just sounds so stupid after a while. I like a guy to have a little class.
> *Monica, 17*

> A guy who only talks about himself and all the girls that like him. Talk about *boooring*.
> *Genine, 16*

> I can't stand a guy with a foul mouth. If every other word is f——ing this and f——ing that, I say to myself, What a loser.
> *Joyce, 16*

– FASHION TURN-OFFS –

Actually, fashion isn't even the issue. Girls realize that you're not going to care as much about appearance as they do—but they don't appreciate a "slob." They say:

> If he dresses like a dirtbag—ugly, out-of-style shoes with holes in them and a sloppy, mismatched appearance—I think... Oh my God.
> *Allison, 15*

> I can't stand a guy with a bulging waistline who looks like all he does is drink beer all day.
> *Marissa, 18*

No guy has to dress like a "dirtbag." Take the time to check your clothing. Girls notice details such as shoes, wrinkled clothing, food stains, mismatches such as dress pants and an old sweatshirt, etc. A good look in the mirror before you leave the house will take care of most problems.

Girls like hard, sexy muscles on guys. They do not appreciate flab and beer bellies. If you've been neglecting your body and you're a little out of shape, don't worry. It's easy to remedy. Hit the gym and start working out. In three months you'll see muscles bulging all over the place. (See Bibliography for a workout book.)

So now that you know what girls can't stand, what do girls like? You guessed it. The opposite of the above. How should you behave, talk, and look if you want girls to be attracted to you?

– BEHAVIOR TURN-ONS –

> He should be himself. When a guy doesn't put on a front, you can get to know who he really is.
> *Annie, 15*

I like the shy, quiet type who will reveal his thoughts and secrets to me.

Dora, 16

I want him to act like he really cares about my feelings and wants to be my friend.

Barbara, 16

He should be lots of fun—have a sense of humor, but know how to be serious, too.

Lee, 15

He should be exciting—willing to try new things.

Carole, 17

The only common thread in all of these remarks is that girls like you just as you are. They don't expect you to put on a big act to impress them. In fact, the act stops them from getting to know you. They don't want you to be so concerned about always looking cool that you can't be open with them and talk about how you feel about things. Confiding in a girl makes her feel close to you, and it helps her to trust you. Being yourself means being comfortable enough with who you are that you can laugh and have a good time no matter what your friends think; you can open up to a girl and show some concern for her; and you aren't afraid of new experiences. Guys who don't think they're good enough to get by without an act are usually the ones who seem hostile and mean or goofy and silly, when in reality they may be sweet, generous, and gentlemanly. What a shame to be misjudged this way just because you're afraid to be your real self—a self that the girls would love.

– VERBAL TURN-ONS –

I like a guy who is intelligent. He doesn't have to be one of those brainy guys—an honor student—but I like a guy who knows what he's talking about—not someone who makes wild statements that have no logic to them.

Deena, 18

His vocabulary should include more than a string of four-letter words. He should be able to talk serious once in a while, not just joke around.

Christine, 16

I like a guy to be deep. If I want to talk about God, for example, I love it when a guy can tell me how he feels, instead of saying, "Oh, I don't believe in God," or "Let's not get heavy."

Rachel, 15

To me, a sense of humor is everything. I can tell you this right now. I would never marry a guy who didn't have a sense of humor.

Emily, 17

When I go out with a guy, I like to talk about my family problems, and I love when he can tell me all about what's bothering him, too—about how he feels when his parents do things to him. This makes me feel like he's not just a boyfriend, but a friend.

Marilyn, 16

It has been said, "The sexiest part of a man is his mind." Girls appreciate guys who know what they're talking about, who can give an opinion about various topics, and who can "get deep" once in a while. Did you ever wonder why some guys who are not so good-looking have girlfriends who are beautiful? It's not enough to be gorgeous. You have to develop your mind also.

– FASHION TURN-ONS –

Girls know exactly what they like:

> Jappy big jeans. Up-to-date.
>
> *Allie, 15*

> I love a guy who wears cologne. That really turns me on.
>
> *Marie, 15*

> A guy should dress classy, tastefully—like he really takes his time.
>
> *Tina, 16*

> He should be neat, casual, and clean. He should dress like a page out of *GQ* magazine.
>
> *Lisa, 17*

> He shouldn't be all mismatched. He should wear preppy clothing, like baggies, a long shirt or a pullover, and nice shoes.
>
> *Margie, 18*

> No specific way, but in style though.
>
> *Stacey, 17*

All you fellas have to do is get *GQ* magazine and you'll have it made. Girls mentioned that magazine a hundred times when describing the clothing style they love on guys.

You don't have to look like a *GQ* model, however. In fact, part of looking good is developing your own style. As a bare minimum, that style should include a clean

– 167 –

body and clean clothes; colors that work together; shoes that aren't down at the heels, three years out of style, and full of holes; and a feeling for the occasion: Don't wear old gym shorts and a sweaty T-shirt to meet her parents. But beyond that, the choice is yours. You can be hip, or punk, or preppy, or whatever. The main thing is to have a style that suits you—and a final touch of a little cologne can't hurt. Girls seem to love it.

– WHO DO GIRLS THINK OF AS THE IDEAL MAN? –

Get ready for a surprise. Psychologists agree that girls formulate their idea of the perfect man by observing the best traits of their fathers. This was true in my interviews, because when I asked girls about what they wanted in a guy, they talked about their fathers.

> I would look for my father's honesty.
> *Adriane, 15*

> My father is kind, loving, and sensitive, so I expect these qualities in the guy I would love.
> *Jennifer, 15*

> He would have to be strong enough to support me when there are tough times. My father is like that with my mother, and he has a very high respect for women. He would never dare to raise a hand to a woman; I think he would rather die than do that. He's also understanding and intelligent.
> *Marthe, 15*

> My father has inner strength, he's a good dresser, and he has a good heart. He's not a Casanova. I demand the same traits in a guy.
> *Lu-anne, 16*

The guy would have to let me cry on his shoulder. My father is like that.

Pam, 16

My father is open-minded and not cheap with his money. I could never go out with a stingy, opinionated guy.

Rina, 15

The thing I like about my father is he would never embarrass a woman in front of anyone. He always treats me mother and I really well in public, so we have a great time with him. If I could find a guy who knew how to do that, I'd be thrilled.

Mary, 18

My father is not suspicious and jealous. I can't stand guys who are like that.

Karen, 17

You have a lot to live up to, because girls usually compare guys to their fathers. You may have heard your girl complain about her father a lot—maybe he's too strict or maybe she feels he doesn't understand her—but no matter what she says, her father is very special to her. Even girls who have fathers you would never want to emulate have an idealized view of them.

When you meet a girl, try to find out what she likes about her father. This way, you can be aware of how to conduct yourself—that is, if you want her to fall in love with you.

No boy in his right mind starts out with the goal of turning girls off. Even mental patients try their best to impress the opposite sex. If taken to a party where they know they will be socializing with women, male mental patients will shower and shave and try their best to carry themselves in a pleasing manner, with the goal of attracting, not repelling, women.

You are not a mental patient (although you may have been accused of acting like one at times). How much more willing and ready should you be to learn how to attract the opposite sex? Why not use your head and learn from what girls themselves say about how they feel.

8

The Worst Thing I Ever Did to a Guy: Girls' True Confessions

Girls have done some really cruel things to guys. You may have wondered how girls could be so cold and insensitive as to treat a guy this way. Well, although it may be hard for you to believe at the time, they're not as hard-hearted and uncaring as you think. Usually when they hurt you, it's because they're caught up in their own problems and are looking at the situation only from *their* point of view. It's only later that they realize how bad you must have felt, and by then there's not much they can do about it.

One thing girls are particularly insensitive about is how hard it is for guys. Guys are expected to make all of the moves, and for this reason they're always running the risk of being rejected. Girls don't often think about this. A girl will react to a guy according to how she feels at the moment. Maybe she was feeling friendly one night and gave you her telephone number. But if she changes her mind the next day, she doesn't stop to think about how you're going to feel.

– WHY WOULD A GIRL LEAD YOU ON? –

Did you ever get the feeling that a girl you keep calling is "jerking you around"? She never says yes, but she never says no, so you keep calling, feeling more and more like a fool and getting madder and madder. Here's what may be going on in the girl's mind:

> I met this guy Kenny at a club. I was in a good mood that night, so even though he wasn't that great-looking, I gave him my number. The next day I was sorry and I started dreading that he would call. Sure enough, he called that night. Now I knew I would *never* go out with him, but I told him to call me the next night, claiming that I couldn't talk. The next night I told him I was being punished. I kept on making up excuses for weeks instead of coming out and saying "I don't like you."
>
> *Jennifer, 16*

Jennifer knows she's wrong to keep the poor guy calling her when she's already decided that she's never going to go out with him, and she's smart enough to know better than to say "I don't like you." Unfortunately, she's not smart enough to figure out how to be both honest and kind. What if she told him the truth this way: "I was in a good mood so I gave you my number, but when I got home I realized I had made a mistake. You seem like a nice guy, but you're just not my type. I'm sorry I wasted your time."

Unfortunately, most girls are not such good psychologists. In that case, it will be up to *you* to get things out in the open. You can help her to stop leading you on by saying something like: "Did you go back with your old

– 172 –

boyfriend or something? If you did, don't worry about it. Just tell me and I'll stop calling. I'm not the kind of guy to hold it against you. No problem." Even if she doesn't have a boyfriend, she'll be quick to take the opportunity to get out of the no-win situation, and she'll appreciate your tactfulness. Of course there's also the chance that she really does want to see you but hasn't had the time. You're giving her the perfect opportunity to clarify matters without putting either of you on the spot.

– WHEN A GIRL TELLS YOU SHE LOVES YOU, THEN DUMPS YOU –

Here's what Marthe, 15, did to a guy—quite innocently.

> I told this guy that I loved him because at the time I really thought I did. Then when he took a ride up to camp to visit me, he bought me this very expensive stuffed animal. I became confused about how I really felt about him. I thought my feelings had changed—I mean I didn't really feel that I loved him anymore, but I wasn't sure. Even though I didn't want to lead him on, I couldn't say anything about how my feelings had changed because I didn't know for sure myself exactly how I felt. When I got home, I realized that I didn't love him anymore, and when I told him, he was furious. I didn't mean to hurt him. My feelings for him had just changed while I was away. I couldn't explain any of that to him at the time. I was too immature and I really didn't know how, but now, a year later, I see that I should have explained

what happened. If it happened now with a guy, I would be able to explain, but it would still be hard.

Girls may seem cold-hearted when they do something cruel to you, but most of them feel very bad about it, only they don't now how to tell you. They lack the maturity or the verbal ability. If you could read their minds, you could find out what really happened and perhaps discover that they were not being cold and unfeeling. But you don't have to depend on mind reading to comfort yourself. You can help yourself by daring to bring things out in the open. For example, Marthe's boyfriend could have said something like: "I'm furious with you because you dumped me the minute you came home from camp, and I'm twice as furious because I drove all the way up there with that expensive stuffed animal I picked out especially for you." Then Marthe would have had the opening she needed to explain to him how her feelings had gradually changed while she was at camp and how she really wanted to say something when he had given her the gift, but was still confused about her feelings.

The bottom line is, if you feel a girl is being cold and insensitive, there's no reason why you can't tell her about it, as long as you remember to state exactly the way you feel and why without attacking the girl. (If you attack and accuse, you will end up saying nasty things to each other and nothing will be accomplished.)

– WHEN A GIRL BREAKS A DATE WITH YOU FOR A BETTER DEAL –

Johanna, 16, admits that she did this out of pure selfishness:

> I made a date with this guy to come and pick me up on Friday at 8:00. Then I met a fine guy who asked me out for the same night. I didn't have the first guy's phone number so I told the new guy to come at 9:00. Then when the first guy arrived, I answered the door in my robe and made believe I was sick. I really felt bad about that later, but I wasn't going to miss out on this fine guy for that creep.

Johanna should have kept her date with the first guy. If the second guy was really interested in her, he would have waited another day or two, and Johanna would have had more respect for herself in the long run. Let's face it. Some girls are looking out for their own interests, and they don't care whom they have to hurt to do it. They feel bad, but they hurt you anyway. If this happens to you, the only consolation I can offer is: you're better off without such a girl. In fact, you're lucky she chose the other guy.

– WHEN A GIRL "USES" YOU –

Tracy, 17, confesses:

> The worst thing I did was to use this guy for his money and his Ferrari. I never really liked him, but he was so available. Then when Jack came along, I dumped the other guy for Jack.

Girls know it's wrong to "use" guys, but they often do it, anyway. Why? Tracy gives the answer. They're "available." The best way to make sure you're not used is to not be too "available." If you have a little more money than most guys, or an extraspecial car, or anything that might attract attention, make sure the girl you date has feelings for *you* and not just your possessions. If you're honest with yourself, you can tell the difference between a girl who really likes you for yourself and one who is interested only in what you can give her. Don't accept less than the real thing.

There's a special kind of mistreatment that goes on between girlfriends and boyfriends. I guess I say it's special because when you have a relationship with a girl, you expect more from her than from someone you just called for a date. So when your girl treats you badly, it hurts worse than it would have if you weren't close to each other.

– I HUMILIATED MY BOYFRIEND IN FRONT OF HIS CLOSE FRIENDS –

Girls admit to being totally insensitive to their boyfriends:

> I got into an argument with my boyfriend because he started ordering me around in front of his friends, so I started saying all kinds of personal things I didn't like about him. His face turned beet-red and he walked out of the room. Later, I felt so sorry about it.
>
> *Jill, 17*

> I was in a wild mood (sometimes I'm very devilish), and we were all sitting outside. I was eating an ice-cream cone, and my boyfriend asked me for some. I couldn't resist pushing it right into his face. Then after I did it, I ran like hell. I knew he would kill me, but it was too late to undo what I had done.
>
> *Monique, 16*

> I wore my ex-boyfriend's sweatshirt to a party with my boyfriend—and everyone at the party kept teasing him about it all night. Now that I think of it, I just wanted to get him jealous to see how much it bothered him, but it backfired because he was furious. I had really embarrassed him in front of his friends.
>
> *Lisandra, 16*

Most people who embarrass others don't plan to do so. They do it because they're completely involved with their own needs at the moment. Jill was furious about being bossed around, and she wanted to get even with her boyfriend for mistreating her. Since she evidently couldn't get away with bossing him back, she chose to attack him by exposing his faults right there on the spot, even though his friends were present. Monique thought it would be a great joke to see ice cream smeared all over her boyfriend's face. She didn't stop to think about how angry he might get or that he might feel humiliated in front of his friends—at least not until it was too late and the deed was done. Lisandra wore the sweatshirt because she only thought of how wonderful it would be to have her boyfriend show how jealous he was of other guys in Lisandra's life. She didn't think ahead about how embarrassed her boyfriend would be in front of his friends, nor did she realize that by wearing the sweatshirt, she would be exposing him to ridicule. If a girl has ever done anything to embarrass you and you're having a hard time forgiving her, try to remember a time when you said or did something in the heat of the moment. Then maybe you can forgive a girl for her behavior toward you.

– BETRAYALS –

For all that girls claim to value openness, honesty, and sensitivity, they can deviate from their own principles in really big ways if they become overwhelmed by feelings. You may find some of these actions unforgivable, even when you hear some of the reasons behind them. You may be able to forgive others. But that's a decision only you can make.

> I went out with my boyfriend's best friend and when my boyfriend found out, I wanted to die I felt so bad.
>
> *Judy, 16*

> I called my boyfriend's house late at night when I knew he wouldn't be home and left a message with his dad saying I didn't want to go out with him anymore.
>
> *Lynn, 14*

> I told my boyfriend I was pregnant. He was so scared, he didn't know what to do. He just kept saying: "What are we going to do? Did you tell your mother?" Then I made believe I had a miscarriage.
>
> *Rhonda, 17*

Why do girls do these things? A girl might go out with your best friend if she was attracted to him but was afraid to tell you about it. You know how that feels. Weren't you ever attracted to one of your girlfriend's friends? The right thing for the girl to do would be to break up with you first and *then* go out with your friend. But even that would be painful for you, and maybe she couldn't face up to having to hurt you. Not that sneaking around behind your back is doing you any favors. Unfortunately, sometimes the force of attraction is greater than one's good sense, and when that happens, other people's feelings are forgotten. It's a human weakness—and, as the phrase says, it *is* human, but it's also weak. Perhaps you can be friends again with the girl (and your best friend) eventually. But you'll probably need a long cooling-off period before you're ready.

What kind of a girl would leave a message with someone's father to break off a relationship? Once again, we're talking about a weak girl—a girl who is terrified of confrontations. She isn't really cold-hearted; she's just afraid. Her fear overpowers her integrity (her desire to do the right thing). She's not planning to knife her boyfriend in the heart, even though that may be the effect she has. She acts that way because she's afraid to face him. She's blinded by her own fear so she can't see how she will hurt *his* feelings.

What kind of a girl would tell her boyfriend an outrageous lie about being pregnant when she's not? My guess is, a very insecure girl in desperate need of reassurance. She is probably trying to test his reactions—to see if he's going to be loving and helpful in a crisis or act as if he had nothing to do with it. By telling him she's pregnant, she's also giving him the message: "Don't take sex with me lightly. I'm giving myself to you. It means a lot to me—and there *could* be consequences."

What's the worst thing a girl did to you? If you think hard, you can probably figure out why she did it. Was she caught up in her own problems? Was she trying to get your attention? Did she want to make you jealous? Was she giving in to her selfish feelings and not thinking of how much she might be hurting you?

When you think this way about the other person's motives, leaving aside your own feelings for the moment, you realize that you don't have to take everything personally. It's sometimes a relief just to know that, because when we get hurt, we tend to look within ourselves for the reason: Is it because I'm so unattractive or stupid or uninteresting or whatever that she treated me this way? But often the way people treat you has nothing to do with who you are or what you've done. Knowing this may not make the pain go away, but it makes it more bearable. You may also be more able to forgive a girl if you understand that she was thoughtless rather than deliberately cruel.

(By the way, you should see what guys have done to girls. In case you can't think of anything from your own life, see Chapter 8 of the other half of this book, "What Girls Want to Know About Boys." If any of the things in that chapter sound familiar to you, you may find it a bit easier to forgive the things girls have done to you.)

9

What Moms and Dads Tell Their Daughters About Boys

Did you ever notice that the girls you go out with seem to be somewhat suspicious of you? Not counting the times they should be (that is, when you really *are* planning something lowdown and dirty), here's one of the major reasons why. *Parents*.

Mothers and fathers, in their desire to protect their daughters from "wolves" and to make sure they marry a man who will treat them with respect, regularly give their daughters *warning* lectures about guys.

– LECTURES FATHERS GIVE DAUGHTERS –

Fathers lecture their daughters about three main subjects. Sex, as you might have guessed, is the biggest topic. They also talk about money, love, and, believe it or not, cooking.

– 181 –

At This Age, Boys Want
To Put Their Hands All Over You

A father's worst nightmare is a vision of some guy taking sexual advantage of his daughter. The mere thought of that happening can raise his blood pressure to the danger level. You can understand, then, why fathers say things like:

> They're all out for one thing. I remember how I was when I was young.
>
> *Sandy, 14*

> At this age, boys want to put their hands all over you and you've got to stop them from the start, because if you don't, you'll wind up pregnant.
>
> *Lee, 15*

> Stay away from them. They're gong to trick you into going to bed with them. I want to meet any boy you date.
>
> *Margie, 16*

> After a boy gets what he wants from you [sex] he'll drop you like a hot potato.
>
> *Stacey, 17*

> If you give it up, you'll be giving up your dreams. Don't expect *that* boy to make your dreams come true.
>
> *Delia, 16*

> Be careful and take care of yourself, because the first boy that tries something, I'm going to get my double-barrel shotgun and kill him.
>
> *Nicole, 15*

What makes fathers so suspicious of the guys their daughters date? They remember the way *they* behaved with girls when they were teenagers. They believe that any normal guy will try to get a girl into bed—and they don't want that girl to be *their* daughter.

Fathers believe that guys will take advantage of a girl sexually and then drop her cold. They want their daughters to wait until they're married because they believe that once a guy "gets what he wants" he'll leave her. This is how it usually went in the fifties. Today, although there's still a double standard, things have changed somewhat. Although guys would still like to marry a virgin, not all guys will reject a girl after she has sex with him. But they do reject girls who have sex with lots of different guys (as you know).

Make Sure He Really Loves You

Some fathers are more liberal. Linda's father says:

> Make sure he really loves you and you really love him. Don't let him rush you into anything, but if you do, make sure you use protection.
>
> *Linda, 18*

Pick One Who's Willing To Spend Money

Fathers realize how miserable life can be for a woman if a man is tight with money. One father says:

> Pick one who is willing to spend a lot of money on you. Don't go for the cheap ones.
>
> *Gina, 17*

Fathers don't like to think their daughters will have to work hard to support themselves. They hope that their "little girls" will meet a hard-working guy who will be generous and loving.

You'd Better Learn To Cook

The world has changed a lot since your parents got married. Women's lib was a relatively new movement then, and most wives still considered it their responsibility to cook a good meal for a man—whether or not they had to do it after working all day long. To most dads, a home-cooked meal is still a top priority, and they tell their daughters:

> You'd better learn how to cook if you ever want to get married. That's what counts after the first few months—a good meal on the table.
>
> *Donna, 16*

– LECTURES MOTHERS GIVE DAUGHTERS –

Mothers' lectures are different. Even though they, too, warn their daughters about sex, their warnings include more details about self-respect, the future, and love.

They Don't Respect You If You're Easy

Are these mothers speaking from their own experiences?

> They don't respect you if you're easy. Every guy looks up to a girl who holds back.
>
> *Wendy, 15*

> After he has sex with you, he'll never see you again, and he's going to give your number to his friends.
>
> *Monique, 15*

Keep your eyes open and your legs closed. Do what I say, not what I did.

Maggie, 16

When these mothers were teenagers, they probably made some of the mistakes they now warn their daughters about—or they knew other girls who made these mistakes. Perhaps Wendy's mother had sex with more than one guy and was looked down on, and maybe Monique's mother knew a girl whose number was circulated among the boys as a "good time." Maggie's mother admits her mistake outright. Perhaps that's how Maggie was born.

Wait, Wait, Wait

Mothers are very specific about when their daughters should have sex. It's never at the age of thirteen, fourteen, fifteen, sixteen, or seventeen.

> No matter what, not until you're eighteen.
> *Adriana, 15*

> Wait until you're out of school and you have a good job.
> *Dawn, 17*

> Don't do it until you're married. Give it away and there will be nothing left for him to know about you.
> *Jennifer, 15*

Are any of the girls out there listening to their mothers? I hope so.

Use A Rubber And Watch Out For AIDS

Some mothers focus on the dangers of having sex rather than the moral aspect of it. They advise:

Use a rubber and watch out that you don't get AIDS.

Cyndi, 18

You can't be too careful. Lots of guys are bisexual and they don't even tell you about it. You've really got to know a guy a long time before you take a chance.

Heather, 17

Don't Bring Home Any Babies

Some mothers are mainly concerned about the problems their daughters might bring *them* if they become sexually involved. One mother says:

Don't bring me home any grandchildren to take care of.

Trudy, 16

No mother is eager to start changing diapers again once their own children are grown up. I've met quite a few high school girls whose babies are at home with their mothers while they are in school. Wisely, many mothers would refuse to shoulder the responsibility that is really the daughter's.

Don't Pick One Like Your Father

Sadly, some mothers warn their daughters against marrying a guy like their father. One mother says:

Don't ever pick one like your father. As soon as a boy says trust me, don't.

Jessica, 14

Obviously, Jessica's mother has had a bad experience—and she passes this on to Jessica. As a result, Jessica will be suspicious of men in general. Any guy she dates will have to work hard to win her trust.

Marry A Man who Treats You Like Gold

Mothers want their daughters to find the perfect husband:

> Find a nice Italian boy who would give you more than Dad and I ever gave you.
>
> *Lisa, 17*

> Marry a man who loves you and treats you like gold.
>
> *Dolores, 16*

My mother warned me *against* Italians. Evidently, Lisa's mother had better experiences with Italian men than my mother did.

Dolores's mother gives good advice. Most girls are looking for exactly that kind of man. While you can't make yourself Italian (or not Italian), and you may not be able to make millions, you can work on treating a girl with love, warmth, and the utmost respect. If you do that, you're more likely to marry a girl who can make *your* dreams come true.

What should you do now that you have all this information? Be aware that the attitudes of the girls you date have been influenced by their parents. True, we are not automatons merely acting upon what has been programmed into us. But everything that is spoken and heard is absorbed and is permanently recorded in the unconscious mind. Parents' lectures form the basis of what girls think about boys, and eventually influences from other sources of information (real-life experience, things that happen to friends, movies, and televisions shows, etc.) are added. From all of these sources, girls eventually form their own opinions of what guys are "really like."

It's up to you to add positive input to a girl's opinion of men. The most important thing you can do is to be honest with the girls in your life. Girls respect honesty —and detest guys who try to use them. It may be difficult to be honest with girls at times, but it will pay off in the long run, and what's more, you won't have to worry about Nicole's father coming after you with a double-barrel shotgun (see p.182). But the most important reason for being honest is that that's how you would want to be treated. And as I've said elsewhere in this book (and in other books): What goes around comes around. It's a variation of the Bible's reminder that you reap what you sow.

10

How to Get and Keep the Girl of Your Dreams

Did you ever wish that someone would write a simple formula that you could use to get the girl you like to fall in love with you and stay in love with you? Well, I think I've come up with such a formula. It's called the "Ten Commandments of Love," and though I can't guarantee eternal happiness, chances are that if you follow them, you'll find your relationships with girls changing dramatically.

1. Thou shalt treat her as an equal and a friend.
2. Thou shalt not use "lines" to get her into bed.
3. Thou shalt compliment her regularly.
4. Thou shalt not be so possessive.
5. Thou shalt attempt to be more romantic.
6. Thou shalt not forget to call her when you say you will call.
7. Thou shalt be more affectionate.
8. Thou shalt not hold back feelings and emotions.

9. Thou shalt be fun-loving and have a sense of humor.
10. Thou shalt not neglect to buy her thoughtful gifts and to take her out to interesting places.

If your relationships with girls have been driving you crazy, it's probably because you've been breaking a few of the above rules. If you dare to take an honest look at the way you've been treating girls, I'll bet you could find the problems and eliminate them. Wouldn't it be worth it if it made your life with girls run more smoothly? Just think of all the aggravation you could save yourself.

Now if you really want to learn something, read the other half of this book, "What Girls Want to Know About Boys."

Write to me and let me know how it works. Good luck, boys.

– BIBLIOGRAPHY –

Vedral, Joyce, Ph.D. *I Dare You*. New York: Ballantine Books, 1983.

Shows teenagers how to achieve their goals in life and explains how to use psychology on people in general, especially the opposite sex, in order to make life happy and successful.

———. *My Parents Are Driving Me Crazy*. New York: Ballantine Books, 1986.

Helps teenagers to understand what makes their parents do and say the things they do and say, and shows teenagers how to talk to parents in order to improve things at home. Helps parents to see what goes on in the minds of teenagers.

———. *I Can't Take It Anymore*. New York: Ballantine Books, 1987.

Gives teenagers advice on how to handle potentially depressing situations. Shows teens how to turn anger and hate into energy to achieve goals, and how to get more love and joy out of life. Shows teens how to find or regain self-respect. This book is a suicide prevention manual. It helps the teen to build inner strength that will stand the test when life's difficulties arise. Gives emergency advice to those teens who are tempted to commit suicide.

———. *Now Or Never*. New York: Warner Books, 1986.

A bodybuilding book that demonstrates how to reshape the body. Although addressed to a general audience, it can be used by both male and female teenagers to build muscle and to sculpt the body. It consists of a four-day "split" routine and requires four one-hour workout sessions per week.

McLish, Rachel, and Joyce L. Vedral, Ph.D. *Perfect Parts*. New York: Warner Books, 1987.

A bodybuilding book that demonstrates how to reshape any one particular body part. Although this book is addressed to a general audience, it can be used by male or female teenagers who wish to work on one particular body part that "bothers" them. Each body-part workout takes about fifteen minutes, three times a week.

Portugues, Gladys, and Joyce L. Vedral, Ph.D. *Hard Bodies Express Workout*. New York: Dell Publishing Company Inc., 1988.

Although addressed to a general audience, this book can be used by male or female teenagers who wish to reshape their entire bodies but who have only two days a week to work out. Each of the two weekly workout sessions takes ninety minutes.

– ABOUT THE AUTHOR –

Joyce Vedral, a Ph.D. in English literature (New York University), has taught English both in high school and in college. She has written for *Parents* magazine, *Muscle and Fitness* magazine, and *Seventeen* magazine, and has been featured in *Shape* magazine. She is the author of fitness books: *Hard Bodies*, *Supercut*, *Now or Never*, *Perfect Parts* and *The Hard Bodies Express Workout*, and has written the teen self-help books: *I Dare You*, *My Parents Are Driving Me Crazy* and *I Can't Take It Any More*. She has worked with teenagers and young adults for the past twenty-two years and has very personal experience with a teenager of her own, sixteen-year-old Marthe.

When asked why she writes self-help books for teens instead of scholarly commentaries on literary works or romantic novels, she says: "There are thousands of excellent volumes of literary criticism, and I think that's wonderful. And there is no lack of appealing fiction for young adults. But after dealing with teenagers on a one-to-one level for the past twenty-two years, I saw a great need, and no one was attempting to fill it: Self-help books written especially for teenagers—books that deal with the very special issues that teens must grapple with and that speak to them on their level without talking down to them. I thought of how unfair it was that there are thousands of such books for adults, books that could help people—*after* the major mistakes were made. But self-help books can do the most good *before* people become adults and their lives are bent in the wrong direction. I wished I had had such books when I was a teen. It would have saved me years of worry and self-doubt. Since it was too late to go back and change what had happened to me, I realized that it was my 'job in life' to offer such help for young people today, and to provide them with direction and comfort when they need it most. I really love teenagers, and when I help them, I feel as if I'm helping myself."

A mountain climber, a judo player, and a well-known fitness expert, Joyce is a multifaceted individual. "Where is it written that we must be one-sided," she says. Joyce is a frequent guest on local and national television shows, and has appeared on the "Oprah Winfrey Show," "Hour Magazine," "The Morning Show," Cable News Network, and many, many more.

Her two favorite pursuits, however, are fitness and teen self-help (see bibliography for a description of some of her books), and when asked which is number one, she says: "Teen self-help. My goal is to have teenagers reach for one of Vedral's books if something is bothering them. The bodybuilding is what prevents me from becoming too intense. It's a great outlet—and being in shape helps me to feel twenty years younger than my age, and it doesn't hurt in my dealings with the opposite sex, which, by the way, is still driving me crazy."

ADVICE FOR ADOLESCENTS

COMFORTING BOOKS ON TEEN-AGE PROBLEMS FROM

Joyce L. Vedral, Ph.D.

Available at your bookstore or use this coupon.

___ **I DARE YOU** 32310-6 $2.50
How to Get What You Want Out of Life
A self-help book designed especially for young adults to help them take charge of their lives by setting and achieving short term goals, managing time more efficiently and developing confidence and interpersonal skills.

___ **MY PARENTS ARE DRIVING ME CRAZY** 33011-0 $2.50
An important book for teens on how to cope with confusing parental behavior. Discusses and explores both parents' and teens' feelings using examples based on real-life conflicts, to foster parent-child communication.

___ **I CAN'T TAKE IT ANY MORE** 33979-7 $2.95
How to Get Up When You're Really Low
A timely book which discusses teenage depression and suicide. Dr. Vedral offers teenagers options and shows them positive actions they can take to alleviate or at least understand why they are feeling the way they do. She includes 30 reasons not to be depressed and 7 reasons not to "do it."

BB BALLANTINE MAIL SALES
Dept. TA, 201 E. 50th St., New York, N.Y. 10022

Please send me the BALLANTINE or DEL REY BOOKS I have checked above. I am enclosing $.................(add 50¢ per copy to cover postage and handling). Send check or money order — no cash or C.O.D.'s please. Prices and numbers are subject to change without notice. Valid in U.S. only. All orders are subject to availability of books.

Name_____

Address_____

City_____State_____Zip Code_____

Allow at least 4 weeks for delivery.   TA-170

GUYS SUCK!